Early SPACE Encyclopedias

ASTEROIDS, COMETS, AND METEORS

by A. R. Carser

Early Encyclopedias

An Imprint of Abdo Reference

abdobooks.com

abdobooks.com

Published by Abdo Reference, a division of ABDO, PO Box 398166, Minneapolis, Minnesota 55439.
Copyright © 2026 by Abdo Consulting Group, Inc. International copyrights reserved in all countries. No part of this book may be reproduced in any form without written permission from the publisher. Early Encyclopedias™ is a trademark and logo of Abdo Reference.

Printed in China.
102025
012026

Editor: Arnold Ringstad
Series Designers: Candice Keimig, Joshua Olson
Production Designer: Ryan Gale

Library of Congress Control Number: 2025939413

Publisher's Cataloging-in-Publication Data

Names: Carser, A.R., author.
Title: Asteroids, comets, and meteors / by A.R. Carser
Description: Minneapolis, Minnesota: Abdo Reference, 2026 | Series: Early space encyclopedias | Includes online resources and index.
Identifiers: ISBN 9781098298760 (lib. bdg.) | ISBN 9798384932567 (ebook)
Subjects: LCSH: Outer space--Exploration--Juvenile literature. | Astronomy--Juvenile literature. | Solar System--Juvenile literature. | Asteroids--Juvenile literature. | Comets--Juvenile literature. | Meteors--Juvenile literature. | Encyclopedias--Juvenile literature.
Classification: DDC 523.6--dc23

CONTENTS

Asteroids often have lumpy, uneven shapes.

What Are Asteroids and Comets?

Comets and asteroids are objects in the solar system. They are much smaller than planets. They are made up of rock, ice, and metal. These objects are from the start of the solar system.

FUN FACT!

The solar system formed 4.6 billion years ago.

Where Are Asteroids and Comets?

Most asteroids are in the main asteroid belt. This area is between Mars and Jupiter. Comets are in the outer edge of the solar system. They sometimes move closer to the sun.

Counting Asteroids and Comets

Scientists count the asteroids and comets in the solar system. They discover new ones and track their movements. These images show how many had been discovered by June 2025.

Asteroids
1,452,096

Comets
4,017

What Is a Meteor?

Meteors are small objects from space that have entered Earth's atmosphere. They are made up of dust or rock. Meteors burn up in the atmosphere. They make bright streaks in the night sky.

Meteors look like quick streaks of light.

Meteorites can be seen in museums.

Meteorites

Sometimes a meteor is too large to burn up completely. Pieces of it reach the ground. These pieces are called meteorites.

Combined, the solar system's asteroids have less mass than the moon.

Small and Large

Asteroids come in many sizes. Some are a few feet across. Others are hundreds of miles wide.

No Two Alike

Asteroids come in many shapes. Most are not big enough for gravity to make them round. Many asteroids have craters. These are from crashing into other space objects.

FUN FACT!

Some asteroids move together in pairs. They are called doubles.

Asteroids may be jagged and bumpy.

Asteroid Structure

Some asteroids are solid. They are made of metal or rock. Other asteroids are groups of small pieces. They formed when objects crashed together. Gravity loosely holds the pieces together.

A rubble pile is an asteroid that is a collection of rocks held together by gravity.

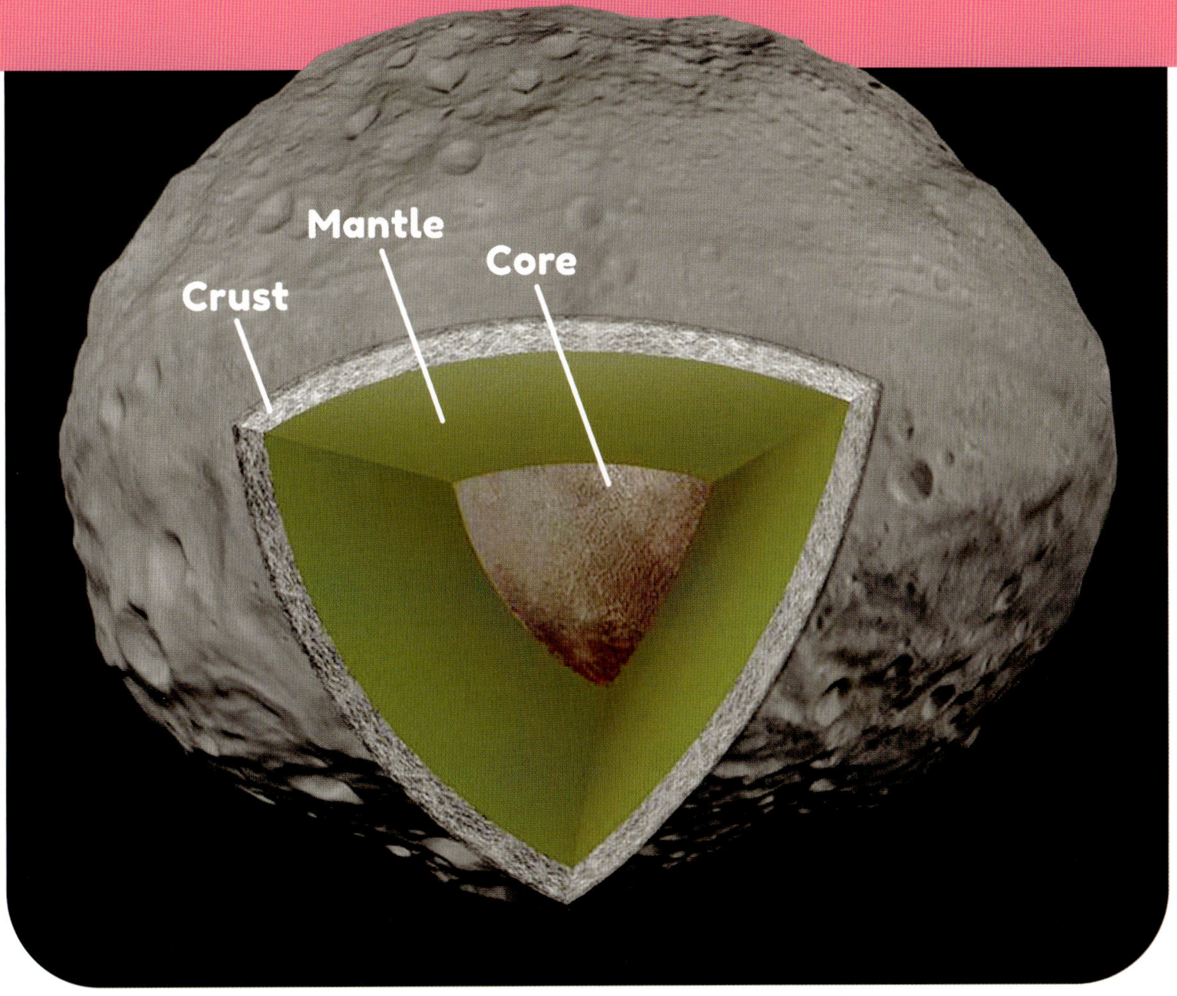

Vesta is a differentiated asteroid.

Differentiated Asteroids

Asteroids may also have a core, mantle, and crust. This is similar to Earth's layers. The core is metal. The mantle is silicate rock. And the crust is volcanic rock. These asteroids are called differentiated asteroids. They are rare.

One of the world's largest telescopes took this image of the C-type asteroid Hygiea.

C-Type Asteroids

There are different types of asteroids. Scientists name these types using letters. Most asteroids are C-type asteroids. They are made up of clay and silicate rocks. Silicate rocks also make up most of Earth's surface.

Ancient Asteroids

Many C-type asteroids are very old. They are made up of things from the start of the solar system. Many are found in the outer asteroid belt. Eighty percent of asteroids found here are the C type.

C-type asteroids contain a lot of the element carbon.

S-Type Asteroids

Other asteroids are S-type asteroids. These asteroids contain silicate rocks. They also have a mixture of nickel and iron. Many S-type asteroids are found in the inner asteroid belt.

The S-type asteroid Eros was discovered in 1898.

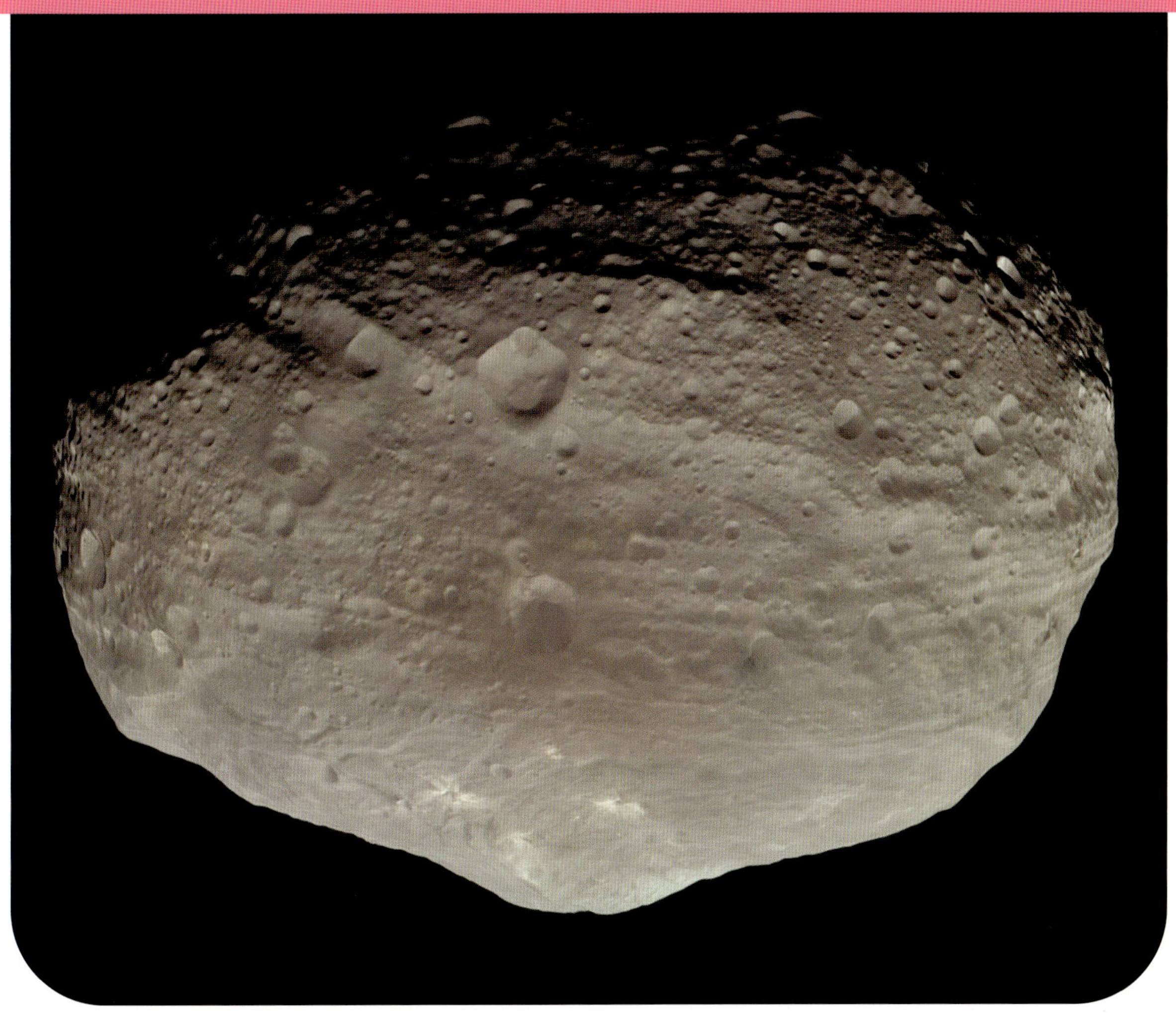

Vesta is one of the biggest asteroids in the solar system.

V-Type Asteroids

V-type asteroids are made of basaltic rock. This is a type of volcanic rock. Vesta is the largest V-type asteroid. It is located in the asteroid belt.

Lutetia is an example of an M-type asteroid.

M-Type Asteroids

Some asteroids are M-type asteroids. These asteroids are made of nickel and iron. Some M-type asteroids have iron cores. Scientists believe some M-type asteroids become metallic meteorites.

Planet Cores

Some M-type asteroids may have once been very small planets. Scientists call these objects planetesimals. These small planets ran into other objects. They lost their mantles. Now, just their metal cores remain.

FUN FACT!

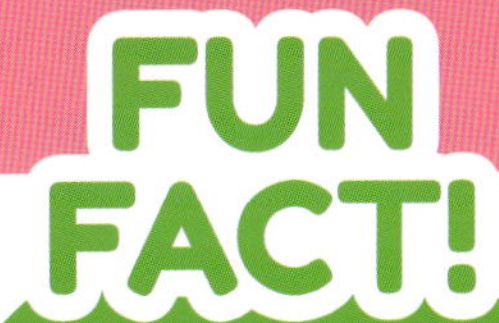

Certain asteroids may have once been comets.

Objects often crashed into each other in the early solar system.

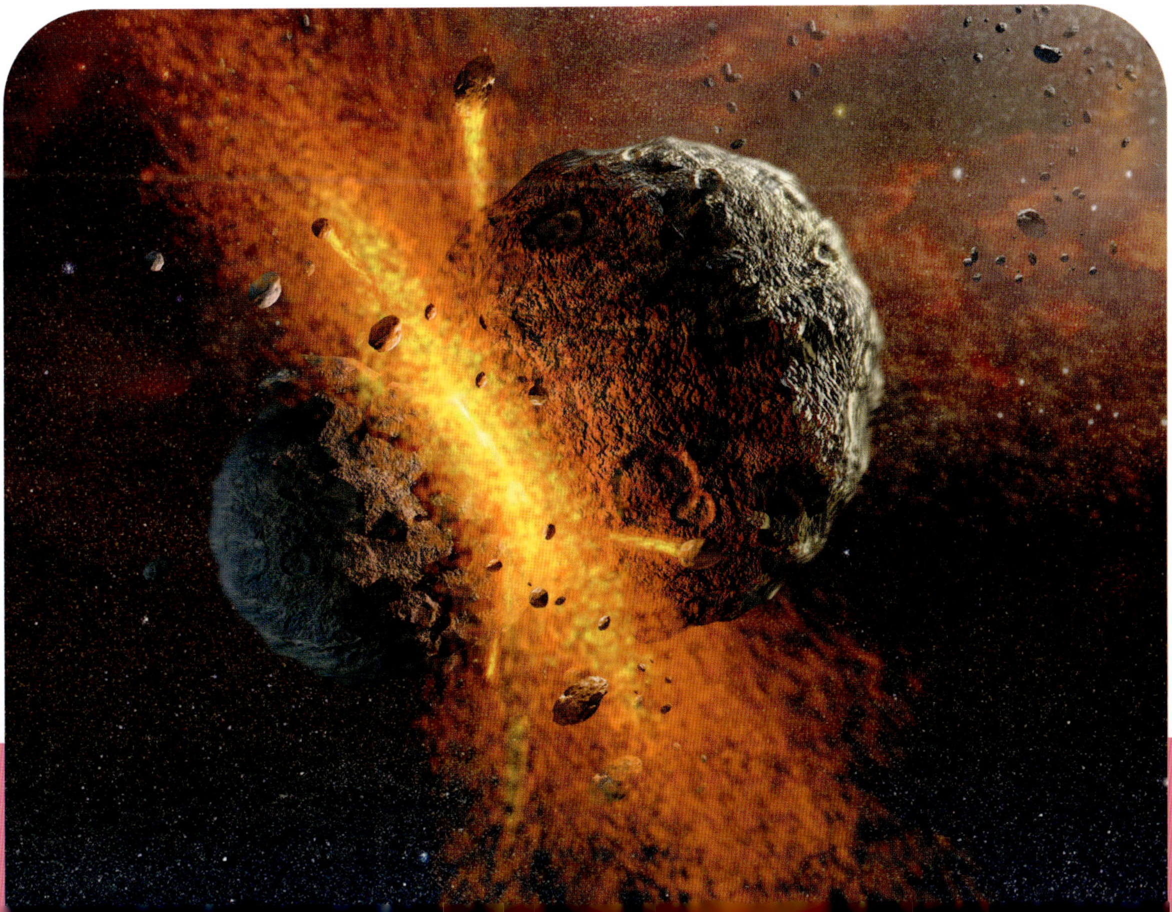

D-Type and P-Type Asteroids

Scientists study two other types of asteroids. These are the D and P types. They are found in the outer solar system. Scientists think these asteroids may contain frozen water. The *Lucy* spacecraft will study them.

Lucy

The *Lucy* spacecraft launched in 2021. *Lucy* will study 11 asteroids during a mission lasting 12 years.

***Lucy* uses two large solar panels for power.**

Scientists have discovered just a handful of dark comets.

Dark Comets

Dark comets are space objects. They look like asteroids. But they move like comets. Large dark comets can be found in the outer solar system. Smaller ones are in the inner solar system.

The asteroid belt lies between Mars and Jupiter.

The Asteroid Belt

Most asteroids are found in the asteroid belt. This area is about 140 million miles (225 million km) across. It contains millions of asteroids. The asteroids in the belt orbit the sun. They travel together within the belt.

Spaced Out

Sometimes movies show spaceships flying through fields of asteroids. They must dodge many asteroids. In reality, the asteroids in the belt are far apart. There are thousands of miles between them.

Asteroid fields in science fiction often look different than in real life.

Trojan Asteroids

Some asteroids are called Trojans. They orbit the sun. But they share an orbit with a planet too. Some orbit ahead of the planet. Others orbit behind it. This distance keeps them out of the planet's gravity.

Groups of Trojans orbit ahead of and behind a planet.

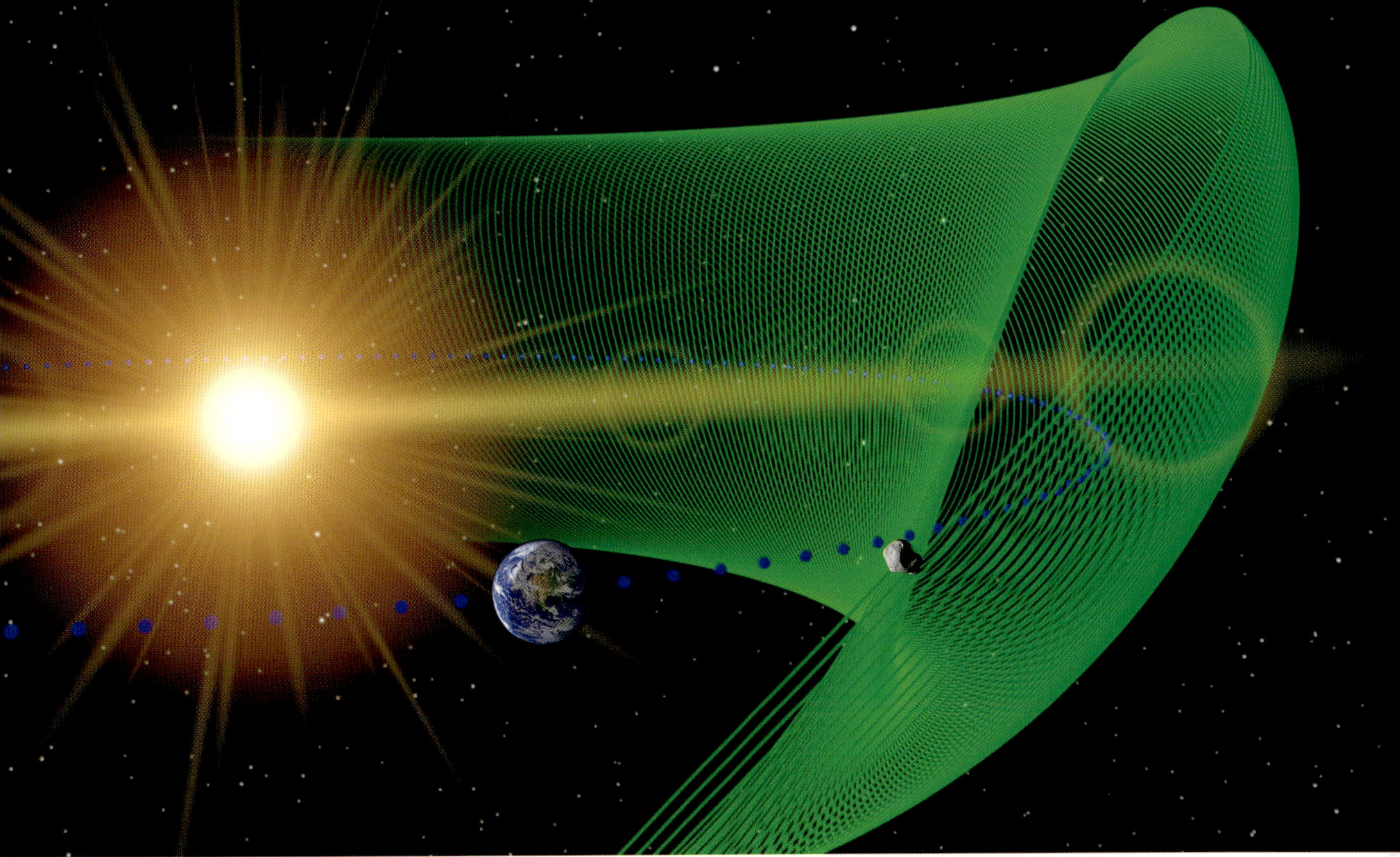

2010 TK7's unusual orbital path, *in green*, keeps it near Earth.

Planets with Trojans

Jupiter, Mars, and Neptune have Trojan asteroids. Jupiter has the largest group. Scientists think it has as many asteroids as the asteroid belt. In 2011, scientists discovered that Earth has a Trojan asteroid too.

FUN FACT!

Earth's Trojan asteroid is called 2010 TK7. It is 1,000 feet (305 m) across.

The Trojan asteroid Hektor orbits ahead of Jupiter.

Jupiter's Trojans

Jupiter's Trojans are named for characters in the Trojan War. The war is part of Greek mythology. The Greeks fought the Trojans. The asteroids ahead of Jupiter are named for Greek characters. The asteroids behind it are named for Trojan characters.

Near-Earth Asteroids

Some asteroids pass close to Earth. They are called near-Earth asteroids (NEAs). They may have once been comets. Or they may be pieces of asteroids from the asteroid belt. Scientists watch these asteroids. They learn if these objects might hit Earth.

Scientists are always searching for NEAs.

PHOs have a risk of hitting Earth.

PHOs

Some asteroids come very close to Earth. Large ones could be dangerous. These asteroids are called potentially hazardous objects (PHOs). Ones that move through Earth's orbit are called Earth-crossers.

2019 OK

Asteroid 2019 OK passed close to Earth in July 2019. Scientists had little warning before it came. 2019 OK was up to 425 feet (130 m) across. It was the largest known asteroid to come so close to Earth.

Asteroid Strike

If 2019 OK had hit Earth, it would have affected an area 50 miles (80 km) wide.

Close Call

2019 OK passed within 40,000 miles (65,000 km) of Earth. This is much closer than the moon.

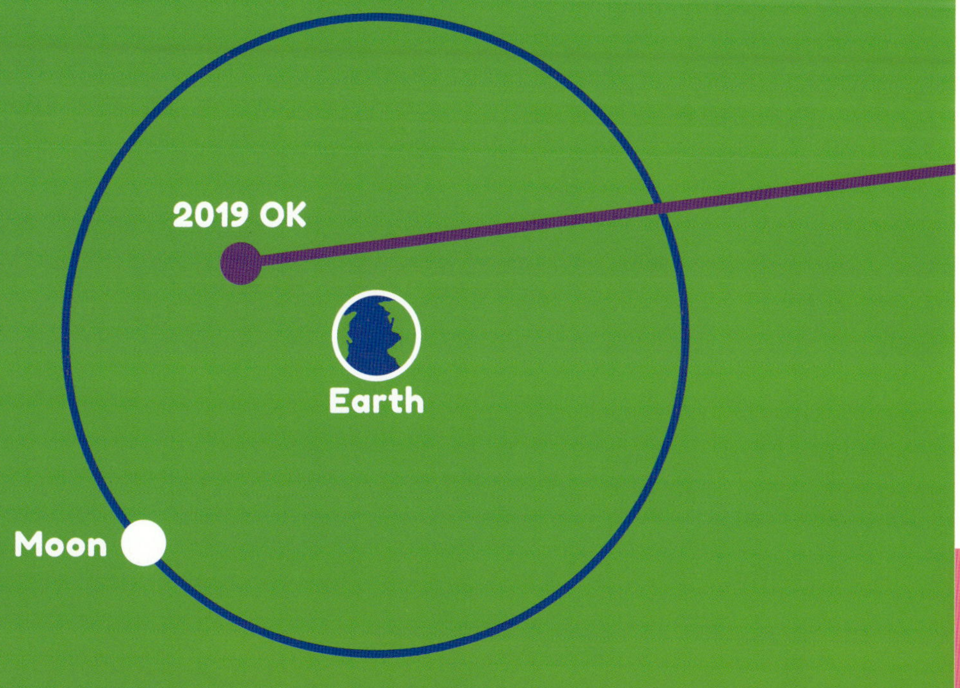

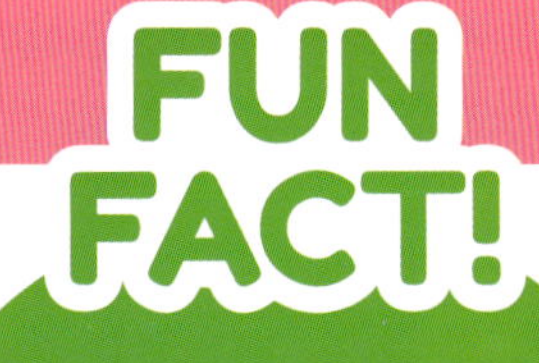

An asteroid the size of 2004 FH passes close to Earth about every two years.

2004 FH

In March 2004, asteroid 2004 FH passed by Earth. It came within 27,000 miles (43,000 km). It was bright enough to see with binoculars. 2004 FH was just 100 feet (30 m) across. If it had hit Earth's atmosphere, it would have burned up.

People can spot the nearest asteroids using binoculars.

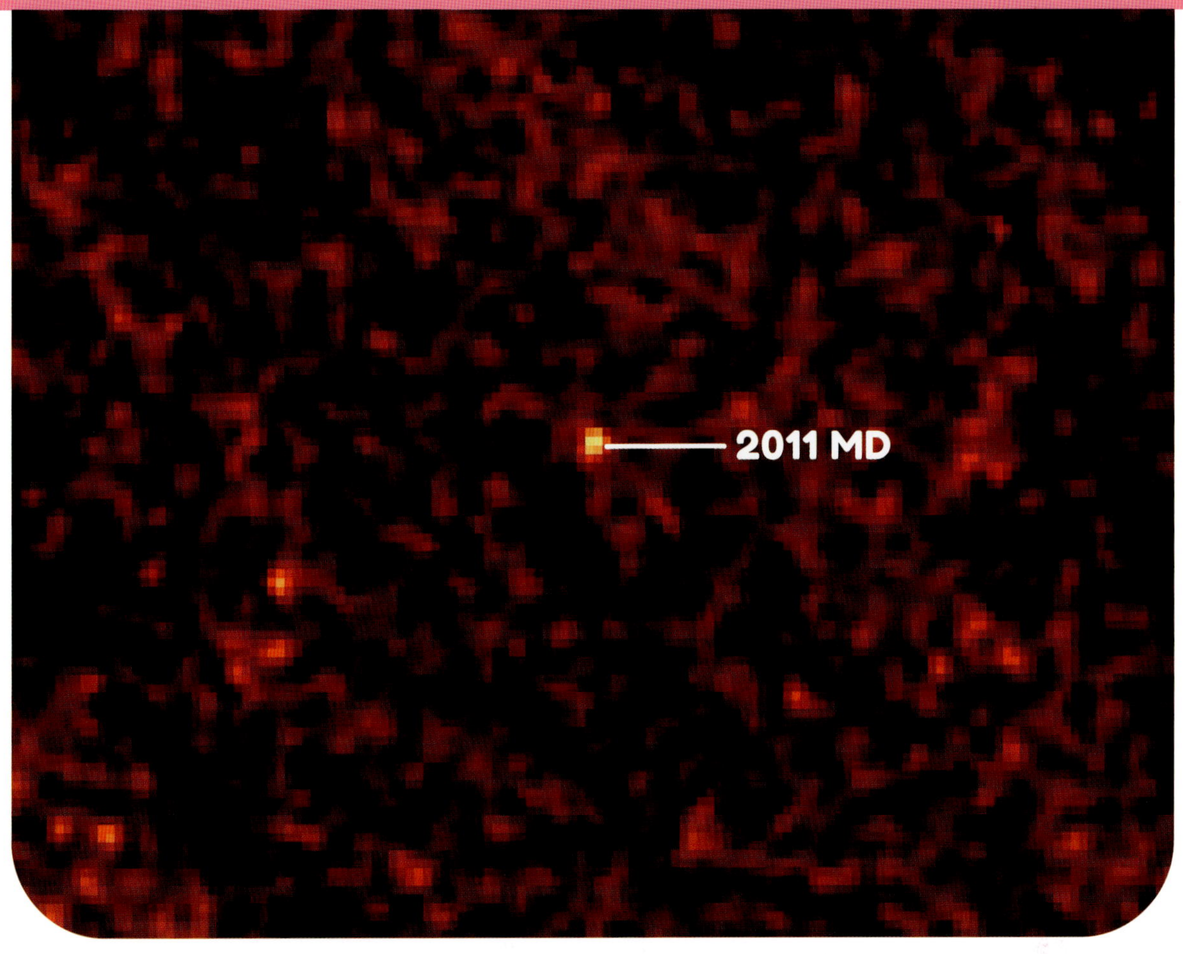

In 2014, a space telescope took this image of 2011 MD.

2011 MD

In June 2011, asteroid 2011 MD flew by Earth. It got very close. It came within 7,500 miles (12,000 km) of Earth. 2011 MD was as long as a bus.

The asteroid 2020 QG barely missed Earth.

2020 QG

Asteroid 2020 QG is an NEA. It passed just 1,830 miles (2,950 km) from Earth. This is closer than any other NEA. 2020 QG was very small. It was only about 20 feet (6 m) across. It would have burned up in Earth's atmosphere.

Apophis

Apophis was discovered in 2004. It is 1,115 feet (340 m) across. Scientists thought it might hit Earth in 2029. But they kept watching it. They learned more about its orbit. They now think it will not hit Earth in the next 100 years.

The name *Apophis* comes from a feared snake god in ancient Egypt.

2024 YR4

In 2024, scientists found a new NEA. It is called 2024 YR4. They found it will pass by Earth in 2032. If it did hit, it would affect an area several miles across.

The asteroid 2024 YR4 is about as large as a 15-story building.

Escaping the Asteroid Belt

A large planet's gravity can change an asteroid's orbit. This can launch an asteroid out of the asteroid belt. Some move farther from the sun. Others may be sent into the inner solar system.

Torino Scale

Scientists use the Torino Scale to measure how dangerous an asteroid could be to Earth. It goes from 0 to 10. Ratings above a 1 are rare.

Crash Control

- If an asteroid is headed toward Earth, a spacecraft could shift the asteroid's orbit.
- The Double Asteroid Redirection Test (DART) mission tested this in 2022. It crashed into Dimorphos, which orbits a larger asteroid called Didymos. It changed the asteroid's orbit.

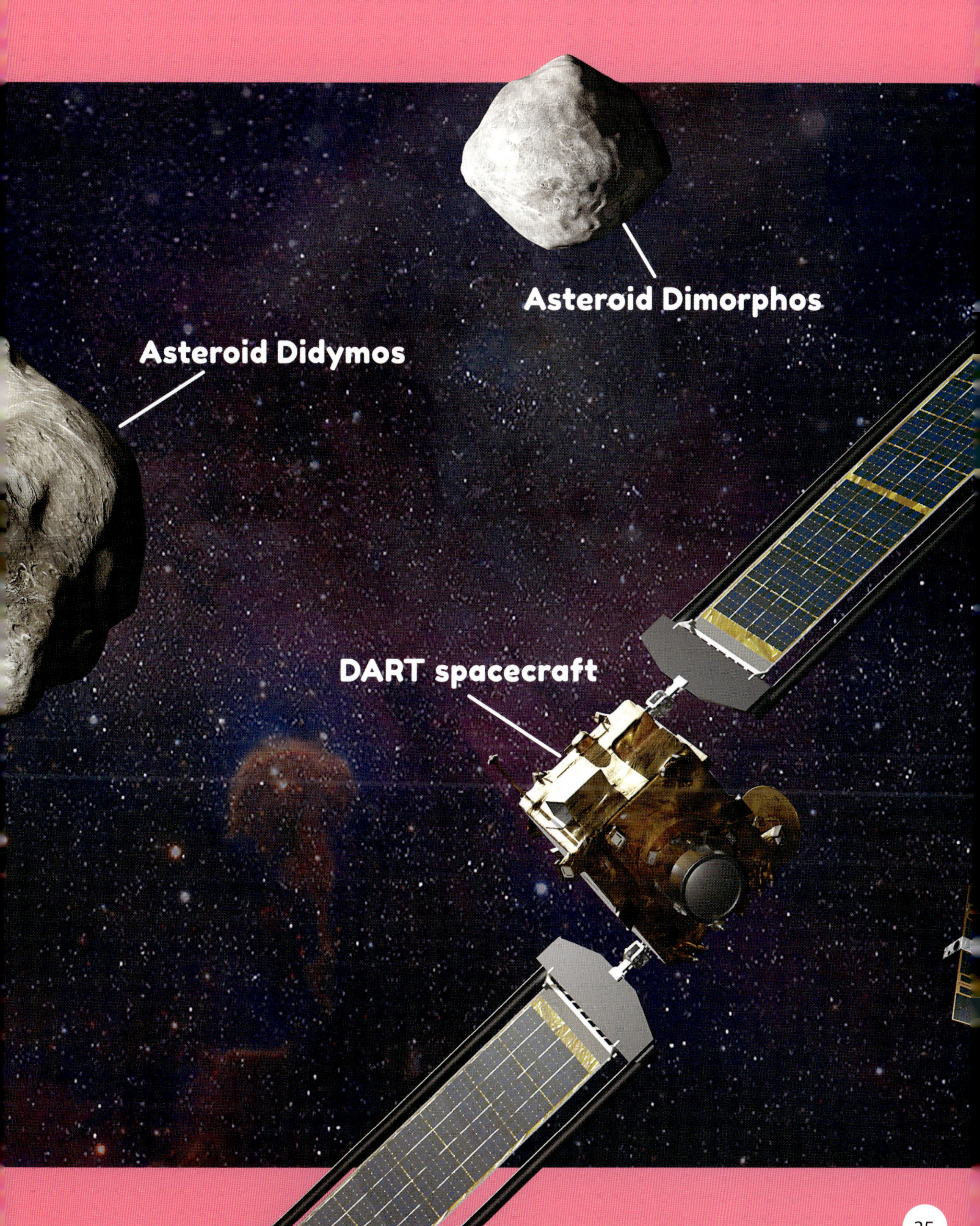
Asteroid Dimorphos
Asteroid Didymos
DART spacecraft

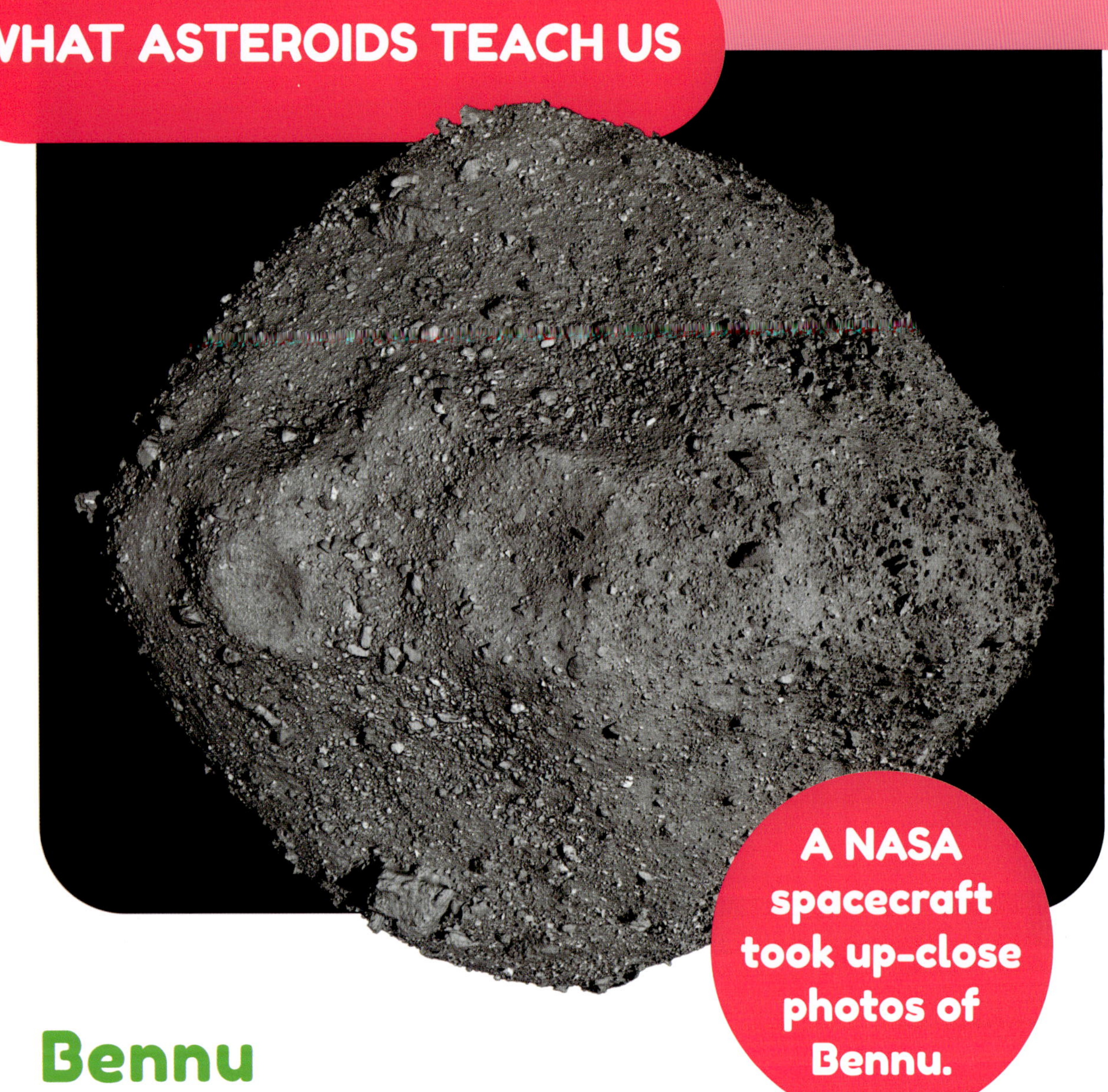

A NASA spacecraft took up-close photos of Bennu.

Bennu

Bennu is a small asteroid. It orbits near Earth. Bennu is 1 to 2 billion years old. A spacecraft gathered a sample from Bennu in 2023. Scientists studied the sample to learn about the solar system.

Life's Substances

Life requires certain substances. These substances include carbon, oxygen, and hydrogen. These substances work together. They form life's building blocks. They were created at the start of the solar system.

Hydrogen and oxygen are the ingredients that make up water.

Bennu's Building Blocks

A cell is the smallest unit of life that can live on its own. It contains substances called RNA and DNA. They tell the cell what to do. Bennu contains the substances needed to create cells, RNA, and DNA.

All known life has DNA and RNA.

Crashes long ago may have brought the ingredients for life to Earth.

Earth and Bennu

Life needs water. It needs heat from the sun. Earth has these conditions. Bennu has the substances that life needs. Scientists think an asteroid like Bennu may once have hit Earth. The asteroid brought the building blocks of life. With Earth's water and heat, life was able to form.

Small Sample

The *OSIRIS-REx* mission brought back a sample from Bennu. The sample weighed just 4.3 ounces (122 g). This is the weight of a tube of toothpaste.

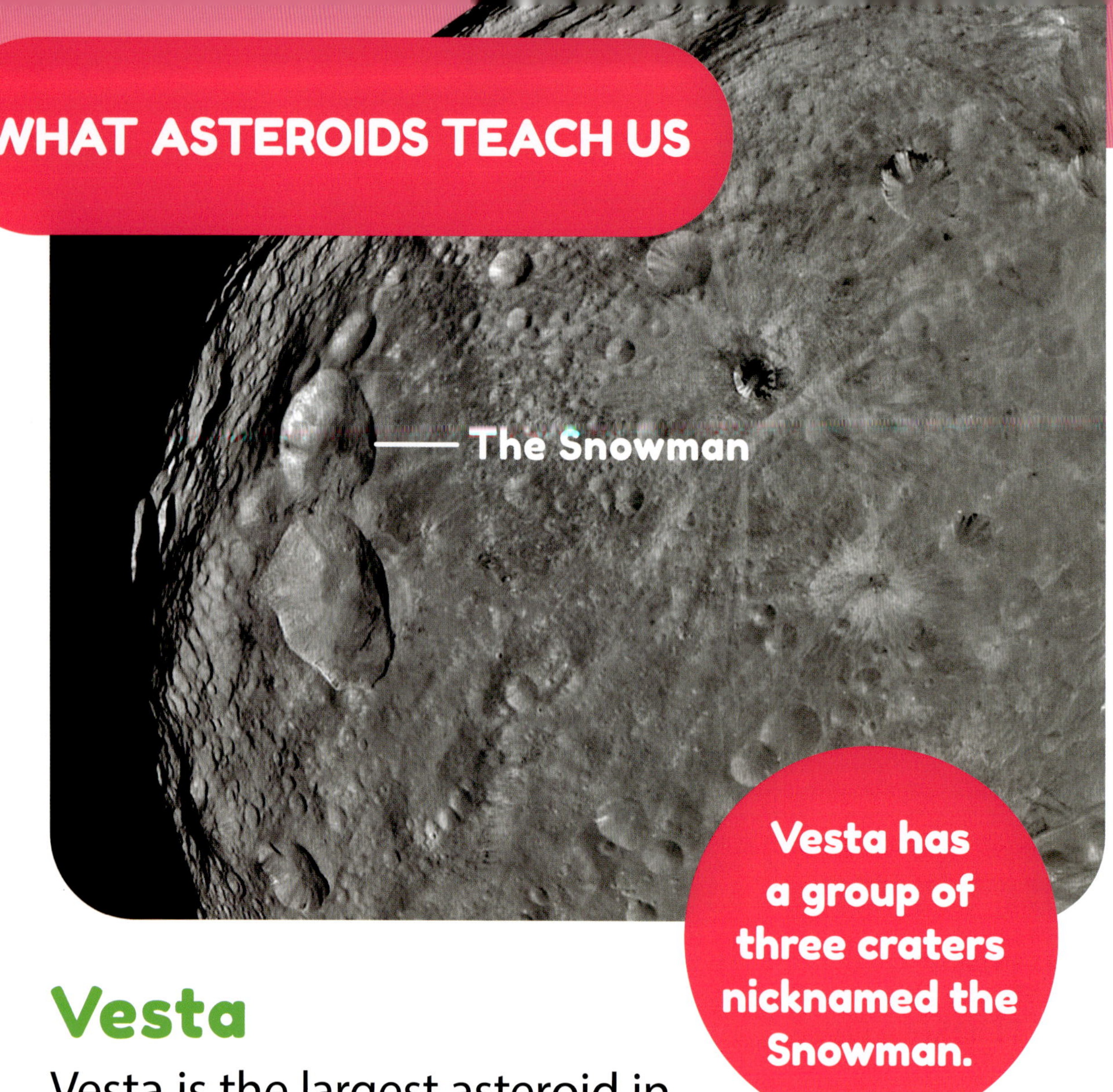

Vesta has a group of three craters nicknamed the Snowman.

Vesta

Vesta is the largest asteroid in the asteroid belt. It is 326 miles (525 km) across. Vesta has a core, mantle, and crust. This is uncommon among known asteroids. Around 1 billion years ago, Vesta got hit by another object. It lost many pieces. Those pieces are now smaller asteroids.

Dawn

NASA's *Dawn* spacecraft studied Vesta. It launched in September 2007. It arrived at Vesta in July 2011. *Dawn* took images of the asteroid. It looked at Vesta's rocks. It measured Vesta's gravity.

Discovering Vesta

Vesta was the fourth asteroid ever discovered. German scientist Heinrich Wilhelm Olbers found it on March 29, 1807.

Scientists work on the *Dawn* spacecraft before launch.

Vesta's Core

Scientists found that Vesta is very old. It formed 1 to 2 million years after the solar system. Warm substances in the solar system heated up objects like Vesta. Vesta melted. Metal sank to the middle. This formed its core.

Studying Vesta's surface helped scientists make guesses about its layers.

Bennu vs. Vesta

Bennu and Vesta help scientists understand the formation of the solar system.

	Bennu	Vesta
Location	Near-Earth Asteroid	Asteroid Belt
Type	C-Type	Differentiated
Diameter	0.33 miles (0.5 km)	326 miles (525 km)
Age	700 million to 2 billion years	More than 4 billion years

Solar System History

Studying Vesta uncovered some solar system history. Billions of years ago, the gas giant planets moved within the solar system. This made orbits in the asteroid belt unstable. Asteroids crashed into each other. Parts of Vesta broke off. This formed V-type asteroids.

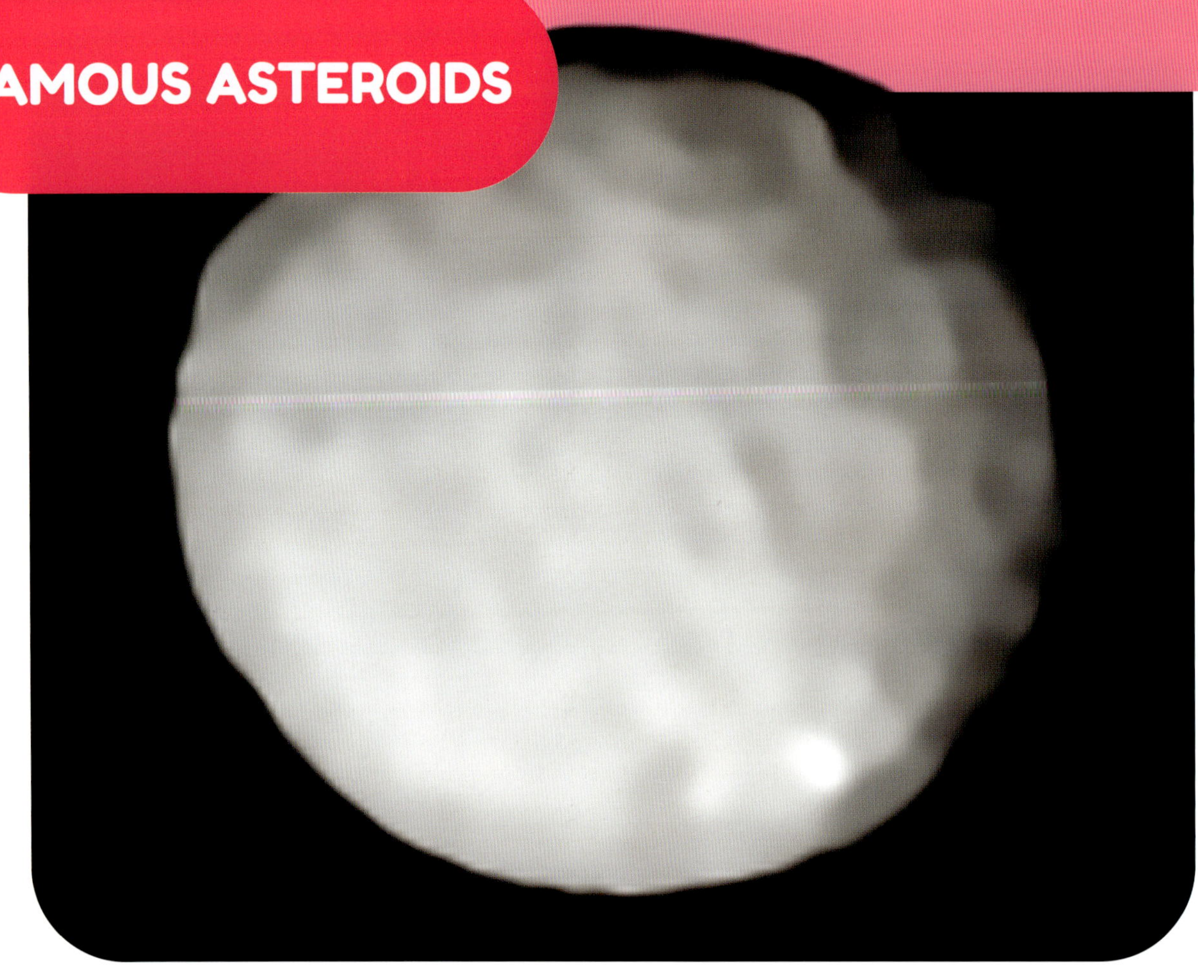

Pallas is small and dim. This image from an Earth-based telescope is the sharpest photo of the asteroid.

Pallas

Pallas is the third-largest object in the asteroid belt. Scientists studied Pallas. They found that it has a lot of craters. High-speed crashes created the craters.

Asteroid Mining

Asteroids contain valuable minerals. Future missions may gather minerals and return them to Earth. Asteroid mining could become a big business.

Eros

Eros was the first NEA scientists discovered. They found it in 1898. In the year 2000, Eros had another first. It was the first asteroid ever to be orbited by a spacecraft. And it was the first asteroid on which a spacecraft ever landed. The *NEAR Shoemaker* spacecraft studied Eros.

An artist's image shows *NEAR Shoemaker* at Eros.

Itokawa

Itokawa is a PHO discovered in 1998. It was the first asteroid scientists successfully sampled. This means a spacecraft brought pieces of it back to Earth. The sample showed Itokawa was once part of a larger asteroid. It is an S-type asteroid. It is a collection of rocks held together by gravity.

Itokawa is shaped somewhat like a peanut.

Ryugu

Japanese scientists sent a spacecraft to study the asteroid Ryugu. The mission returned a sample to Earth. Like Bennu, Ryugu has some substances needed for life. But the sample did not include substances needed to create DNA and RNA.

A NASA illustration shows what Psyche might look like.

Psyche

Psyche is an M-type asteroid. It is rich in iron and nickel, similar to Earth's core. Scientists think it may be the core of an old planet. They think other asteroids hit Psyche. This wore away its rocky crust and mantle. Psyche could show scientists how Earth's core formed.

Ida and Dactyl

Ida and its moon, Dactyl, are in the asteroid belt. Ida is an S-type asteroid. It is mostly silicate rock. Ida is the first known asteroid with a moon.

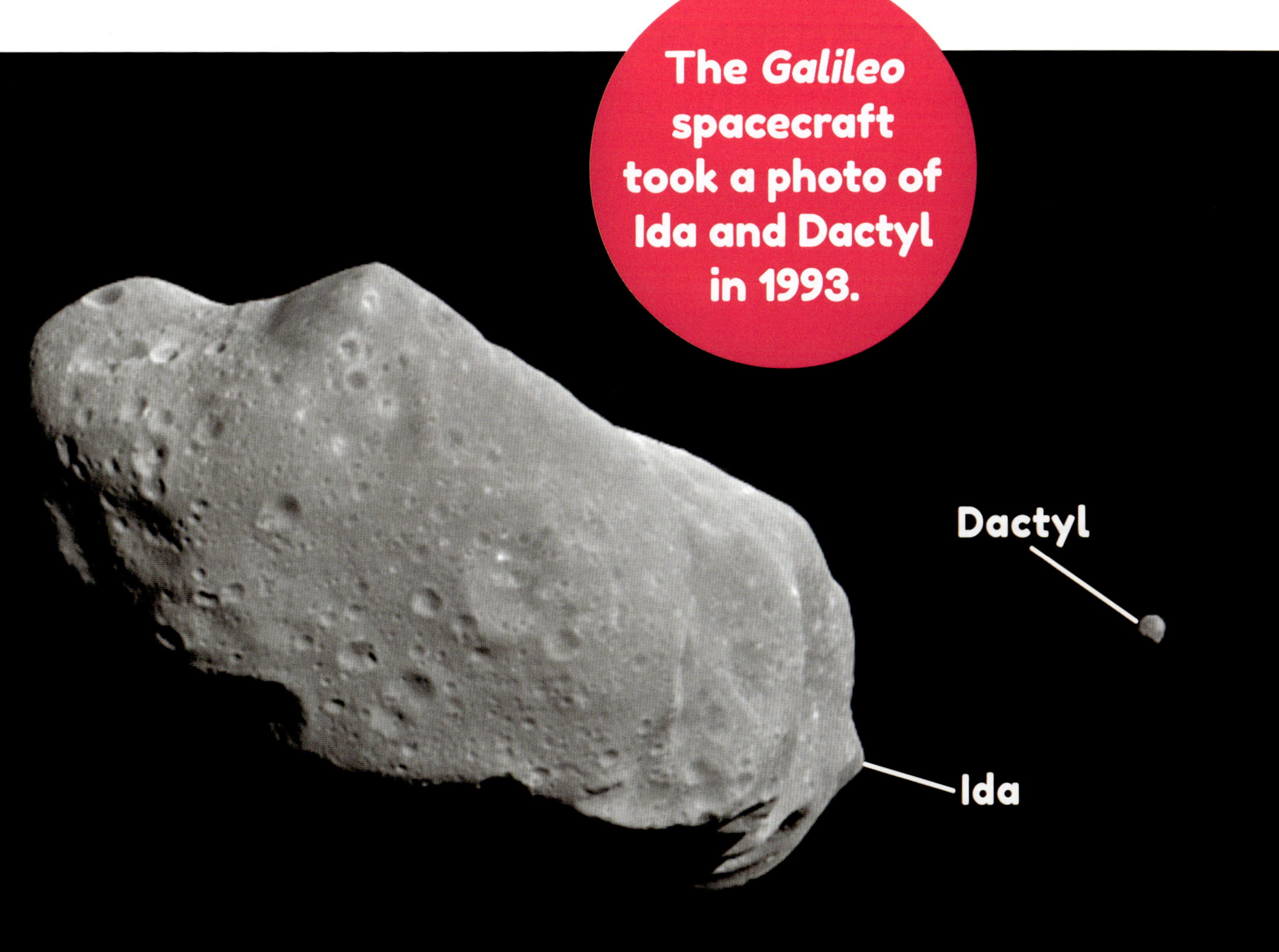

Didymos and Dimorphos

Like Ida, Didymos has a moon. Dimorphos orbits around Didymos. They are NEAs. NASA sent the DART mission to them. It wanted to test out changing an asteroid's orbit. DART hit Dimorphos at a speed of 4 miles per second (6.4 km/s). The test worked. The orbit of Dimorphos changed.

This is the final full photo DART took before hitting the asteroid.

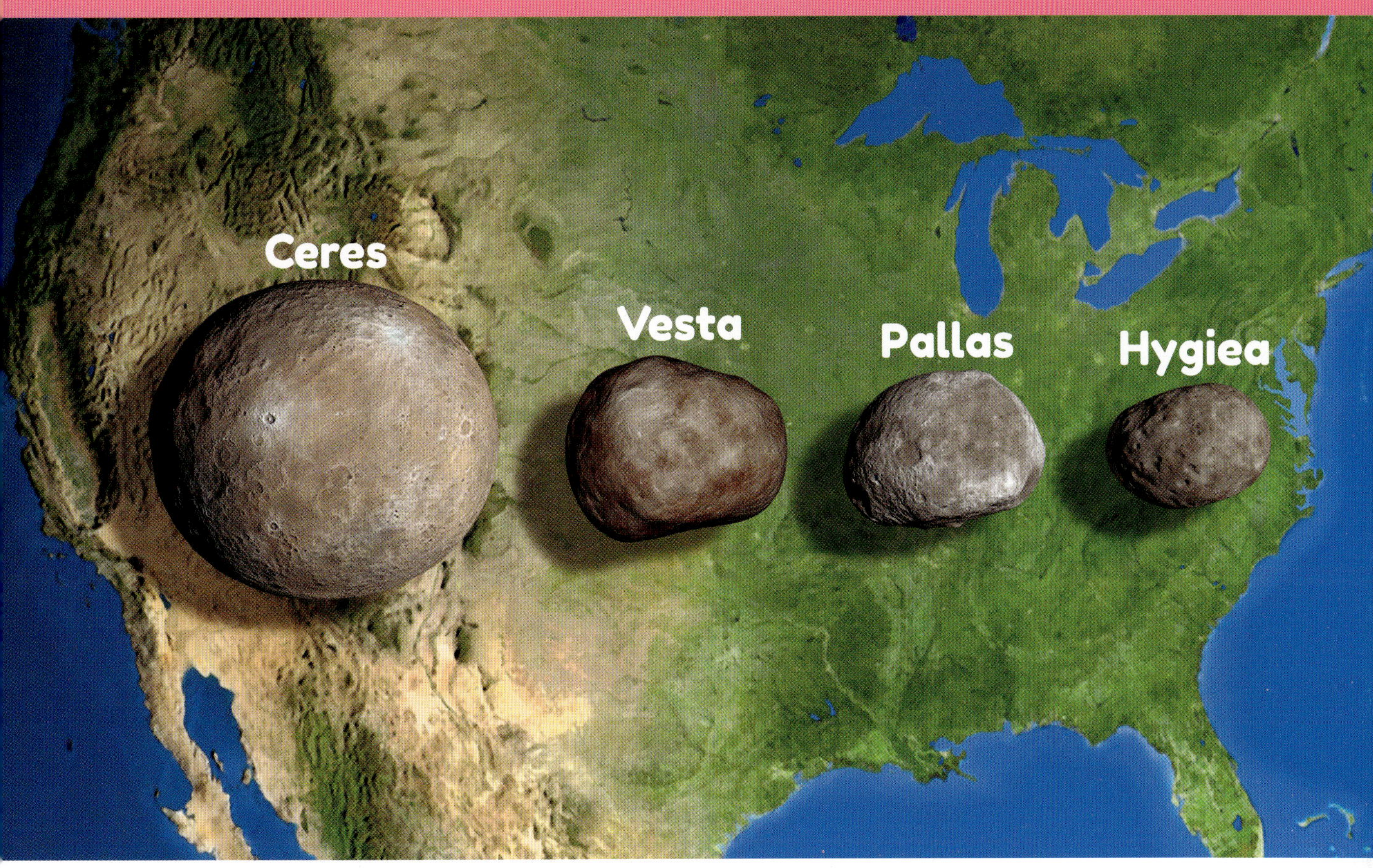

This image shows the sizes of Ceres and the three largest asteroids.

Ceres

Ceres is the largest object in the asteroid belt. It was once considered an asteroid. But today scientists call it a dwarf planet. It is much bigger than other belt objects. Scientists think Ceres has a solid core. They think it has an icy mantle.

Comet nuclei are sometimes known as dirty snowballs.

Comet Nucleus

The core of a comet is called the nucleus. It is made of solid ice, gases, rock, and dust. In the outer solar system, the nucleus is all a comet has.

Nucleus Sizes

Comets are large space objects. A nucleus may be a few miles across. This is the size of a small town. Others are tens of miles across. This is the size of a big city.

The nucleus of comet Tempel 1 is about 3.7 miles (6 km) wide.

Fuzzy Cloud

Gravity pulls comets closer to the sun. The nucleus heats up. The ice melts. Water, gases, and dust are pushed out. They form a fuzzy cloud around the nucleus.

Things coming off a comet make it possible for people to see it.

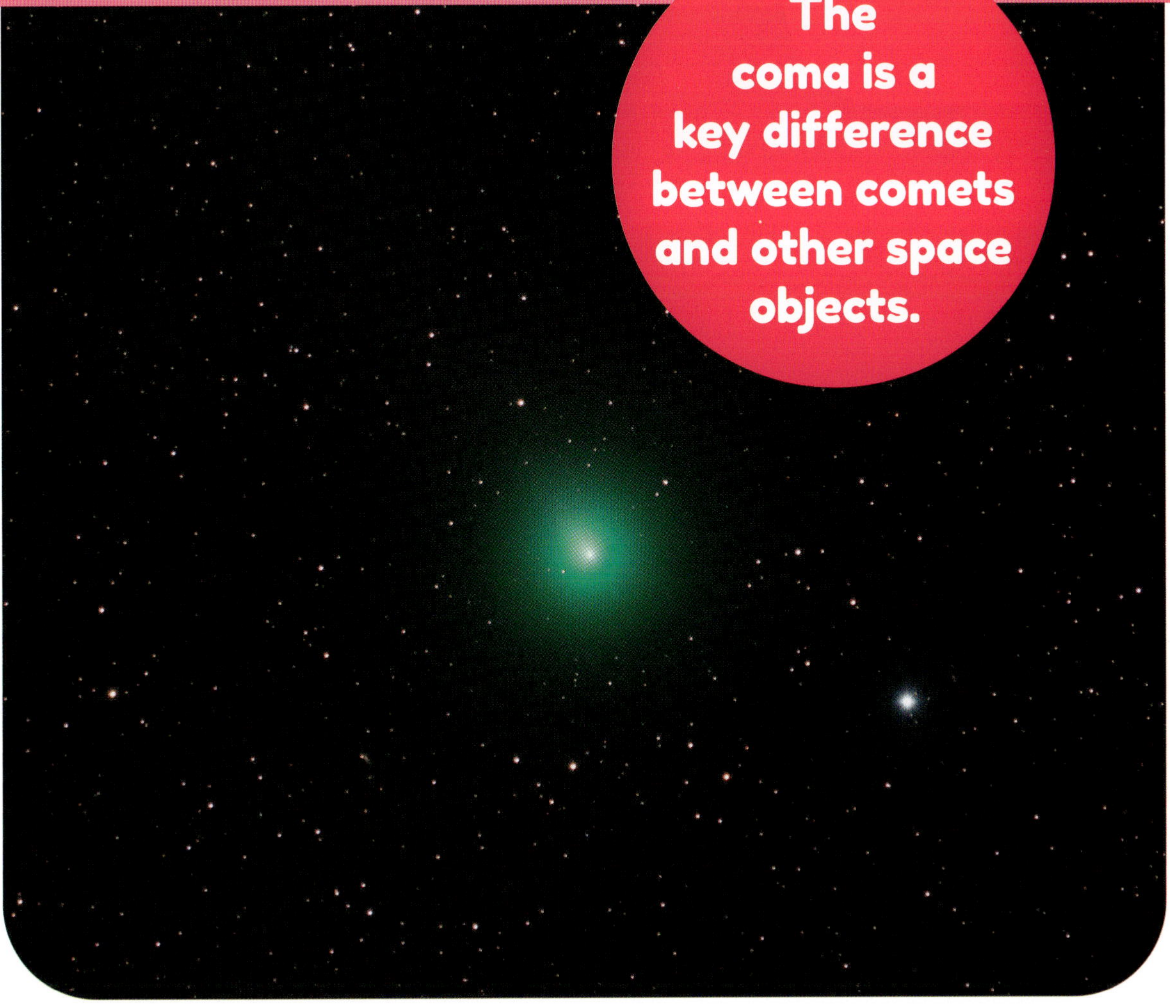

The coma is a key difference between comets and other space objects.

Comet Coma

A comet's fuzzy cloud is called a coma. A comet's coma can become very large. It grows as the comet gets closer to the sun.

FUN FACT!

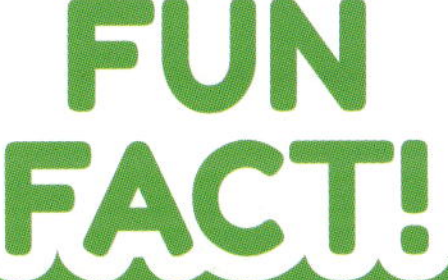

Sunlight reflects off the coma, making comets visible.

A comet's tail may stretch for millions of miles.

Comet Tail

The coma grows. The outer edge forms two tails. The dust tail is dust from the nucleus. The ion tail contains gas from the nucleus. It is a bluish color. Ions are particles with an electric charge.

Two Directions

A comet's tails point in two directions. The dust tail follows the comet's motion. It trails behind the comet as it moves around the sun. The ion tail always points away from the sun.

Parts of a Comet

A comet has a nucleus, a coma, and two tails.

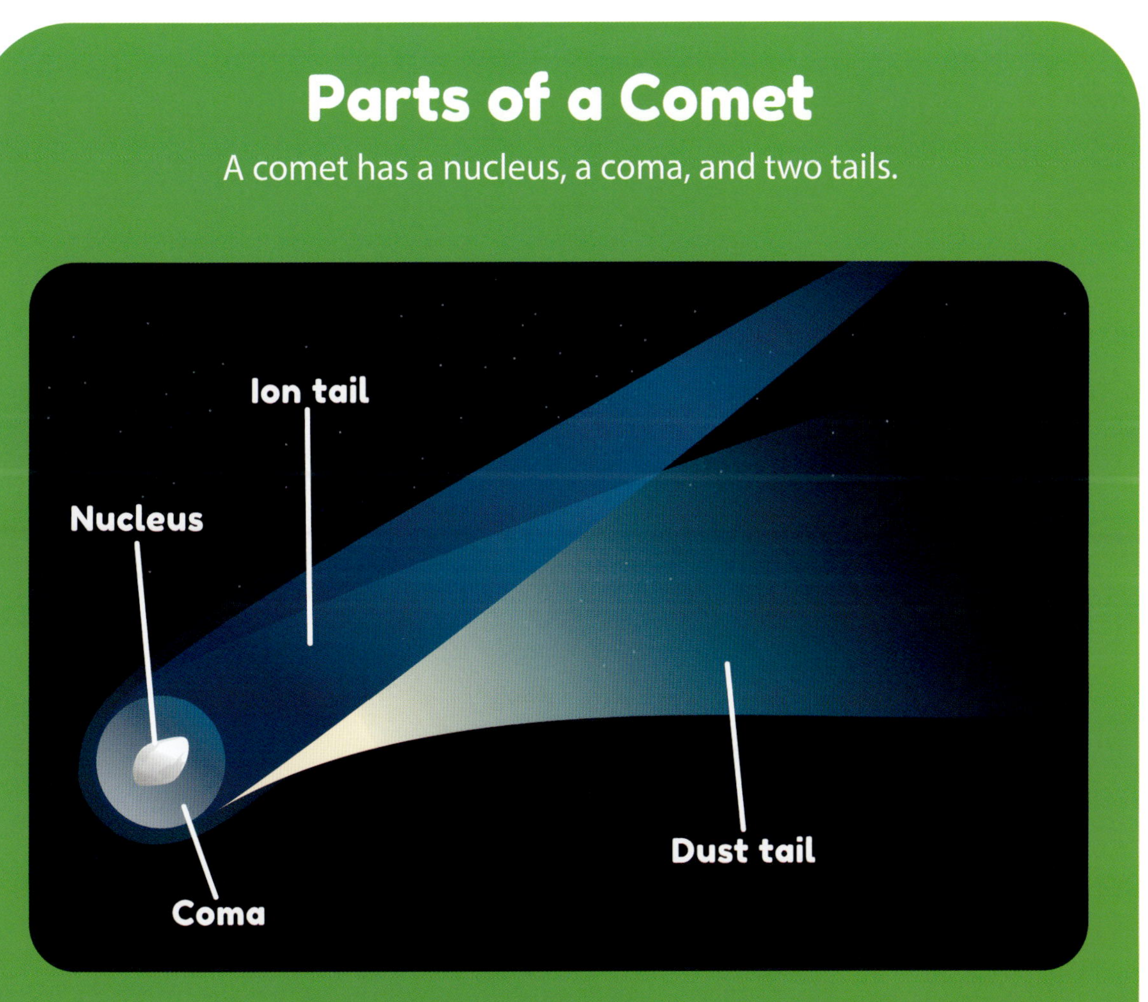

What Is in a Comet?

Comets are made up of ice and frozen gases. A comet's nucleus is up to 80 percent ice. It also contains frozen carbon monoxide and carbon dioxide. It has ammonia and methanol too.

Only a few spacecraft have taken up-close photos of comets.

The things coming from a comet may contain clues to the past.

Ancient Substances

Comets also contain dust and rock. These substances are from the very start of the solar system. Studying comets helps scientists understand the early solar system.

An artist's image shows *Stardust* catching up with Wild 2.

Stardust Mission

The *Stardust* mission studied a comet. It was the first spacecraft to collect samples from a comet. It came near the comet Wild 2. The spacecraft took substances from the coma. Then it returned to Earth.

Comet Names

Comets are named after their discoverers. This may be a person. It could also be a spacecraft. Wild 2 is named for astronomer Paul Wild.

Mission Findings

Scientists studied the sample. They found many hydrocarbons. These are the building blocks of life. The *Stardust* mission also found minerals. These minerals originally formed near the sun. This told scientists that substances could travel across the solar system.

***Stardust*'s sturdy sample return capsule landed in a desert in Utah.**

Comets in Orbit

Comets move around the sun. They move along a regular path. This path is an orbit. A comet does not orbit in a perfect circle. It moves in an ellipse. An ellipse looks like an oval or egg.

A comet's distance from the sun can vary greatly over time.

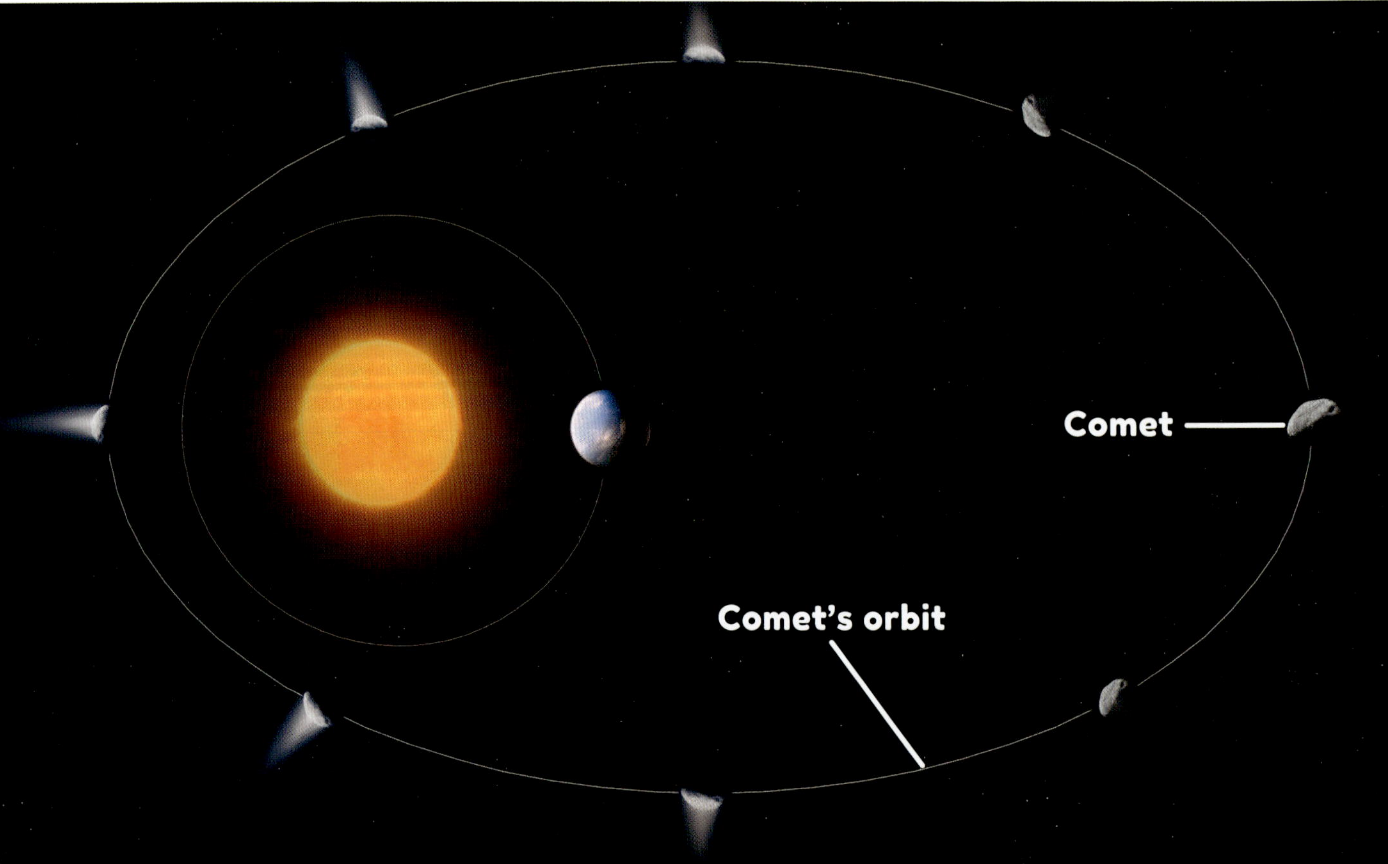

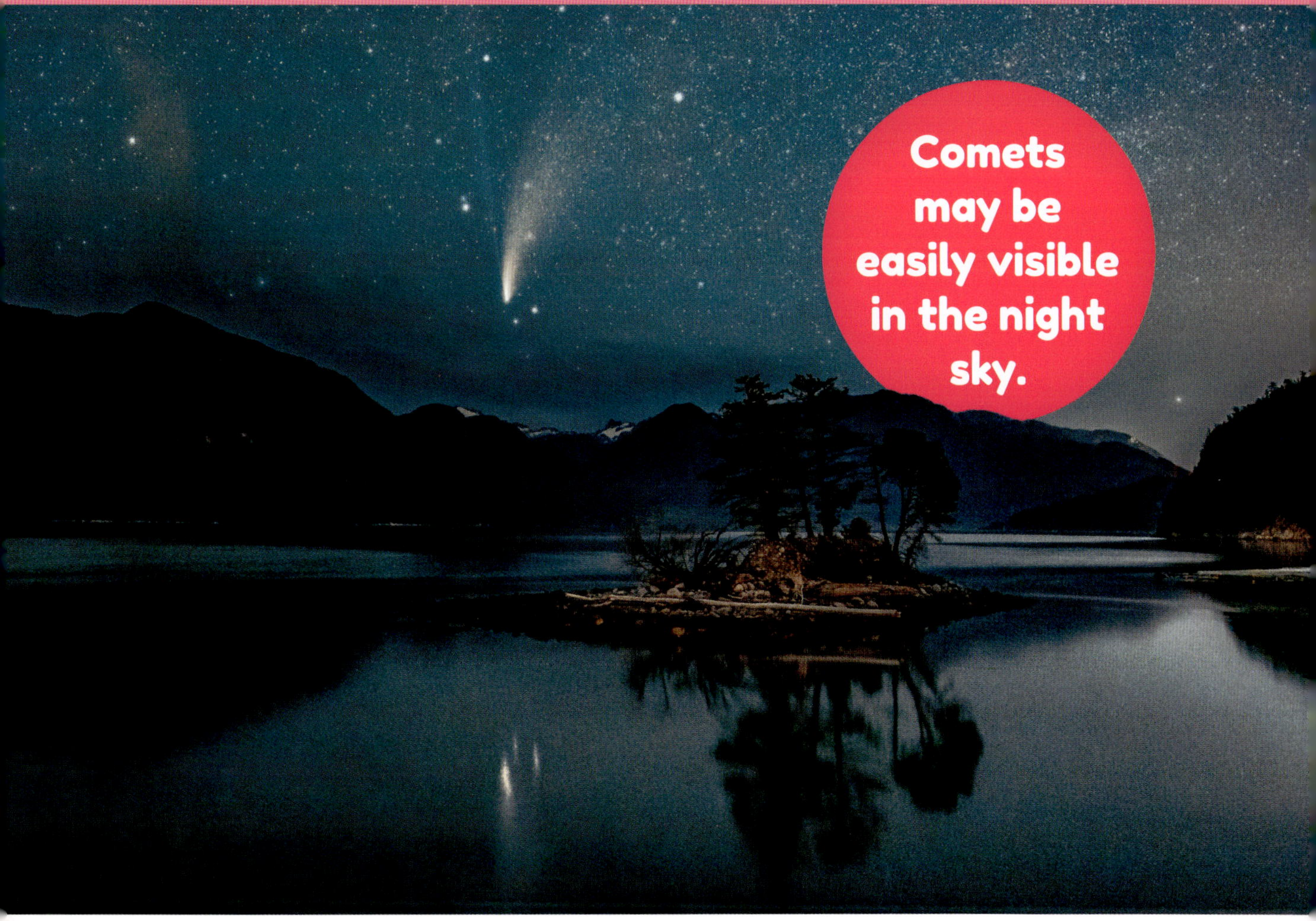

Comets may be easily visible in the night sky.

Comets and the Sun

As a comet gets closer to the sun, it heats up. It gives off gases and dust. This makes the comet glow. It becomes visible from Earth.

FUN FACT!

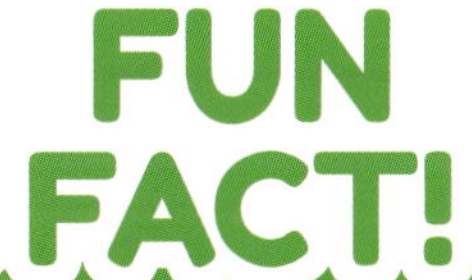

Billions of comets likely exist in the outer solar system.

Astronomers saw a non-periodic comet in 1577.

Periodic vs. Non-Periodic

Some comets are periodic. This means they return to the inner solar system. Their orbits take less than 200 years to complete. All others are non-periodic. They may not return to the inner solar system. Or their orbits may take more than 200 years.

The Kuiper Belt

Some comets orbit the sun in the Kuiper Belt. This is a large area in space. It is shaped like a doughnut. The Kuiper Belt is far out in the solar system. It is beyond the planet Neptune.

The Kuiper Belt includes the dwarf planet Pluto.

Kuiper Belt Objects

Billions of comets exist in the Kuiper Belt. Most are icy bodies. They have been there since the start of the solar system. Together, they orbit the sun.

Kuiper Belt objects are very far from the sun.

A planet's gravity can pull comets toward the sun.

Powerful Gravity

Some comets are pulled into Neptune's orbit. Others are pulled into Jupiter's orbit. These planets are huge. Their gravity moves objects out of the Kuiper Belt.

FUN FACT!

The Kuiper Belt object Arrokoth is the most distant object ever visited by a spacecraft.

The Oort Cloud extends very far beyond the planets.

The Oort Cloud

Some comets orbit the sun in the Oort Cloud. This region is in the outer solar system. It is far beyond the Kuiper Belt. The cloud is thousands of astronomical units (AU) wide. One AU is the distance between Earth and the sun. It is about 93 million miles (150 million km).

Solar System Bubble

The Oort Cloud is like a big, thick bubble. It surrounds the entire solar system. It is filled with icy, comet-like objects. Scientists think there may be billions or trillions of objects there.

The Oort Cloud is so distant that it is hard to discover objects there.

Oort Cloud Orbits

The orbits of objects in the Oort Cloud may change. Objects may crash into each other. This can send an object on a new path. It may cross close to Earth and other planets.

Crashes can change the paths of objects in deep space.

In 2024, scientists spotted a comet on its way out of the solar system.

Escaping the Solar System

Sometimes, a comet escapes the solar system. A crash may knock it into deep space. Other times, a planet's gravity pulls on a comet. It slingshots the comet out of the solar system.

Lexell's Comet was one of the closest comets ever.

Lexell's Comet

Some comets get close to Earth. In 1770, Lexell's Comet came very near. It got within 0.015 AU of Earth. This is just five times farther away than the moon.

Near-Earth Objects

Scientists classify Lexell's Comet as a near-Earth object (NEO). They track the movements of NEOs. They learn when the NEOs will come close to Earth. Scientists do not believe Lexell's Comet is dangerous to the planet.

The *WISE* spacecraft has helped search for NEOs.

Comet IRAS-Araki-Alcock

Comet IRAS-Araki-Alcock is another NEO. Scientists watched it on May 11, 1983. The comet got close to Earth. It came within 0.031 AU of the planet. Only Lexell's Comet has come closer.

Comet IRAS-Araki-Alcock is named for the IRAS space telescope and two astronomers.

Comets spend much of their time in cold, dark space far from the sun.

Non-Periodic Comet

IRAS-Araki-Alcock is a non-periodic comet. It will come close to Earth again. But that will take centuries. It will not pass by Earth for another 900 years.

Halley's Comet

Halley's Comet is the most famous comet. It is visible every 76 years. People have seen it for more than 2,000 years. Halley's Comet is 9 miles (14.5 km) long. It is shaped like a potato. It last passed Earth in 1986. It will come back in 2061.

Halley's Comet Orbit

The orbit of Halley's Comet is a long oval shape that brings it close to the sun and then far from the sun.

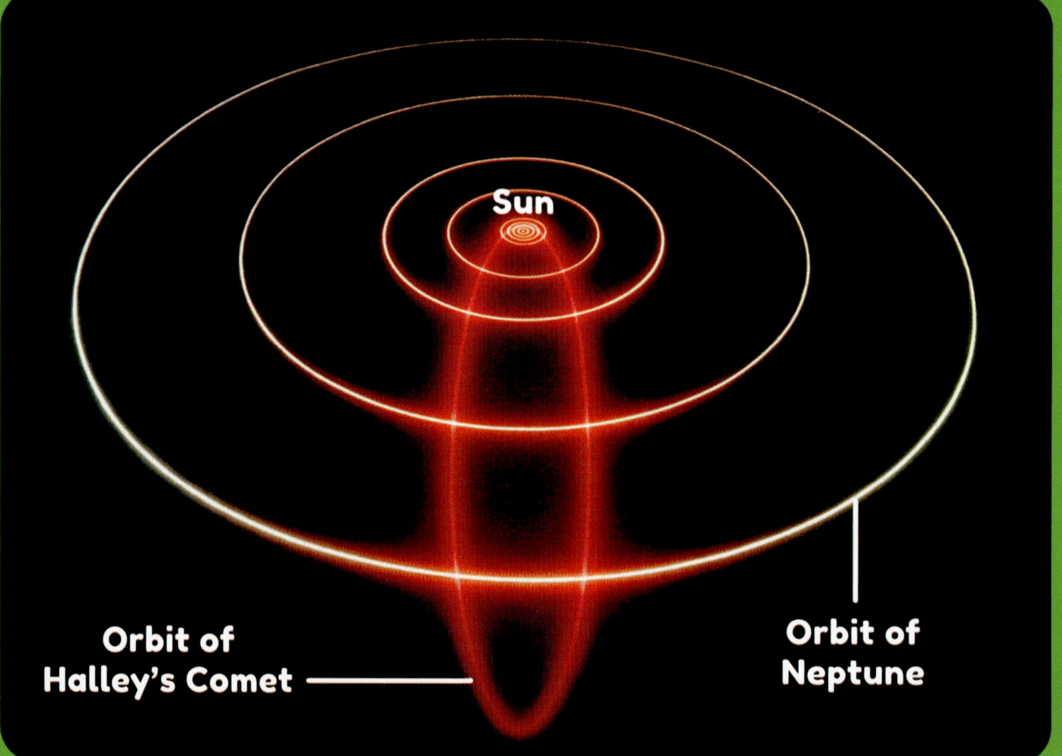

An artist's image shows the 1994 comet hitting Jupiter.

Comet Shoemaker-Levy 9

Shoemaker-Levy 9 was seen in 1994. Jupiter's gravity ripped the comet apart. Its parts hit Jupiter in at least 21 places. This created fireballs. The largest fireball rose 1,800 miles (2,900 km) above Jupiter's clouds.

Astronauts took photos of Hale-Bopp from orbit.

Comet Hale-Bopp

The Hale-Bopp comet went past Earth in 1997. It came within 1.3 AU. Its nucleus was 37 miles (60 km) across. It gave off a lot of dust and gas. This made the comet bright to the naked eye.

Comet Hyakutake

Comet Hyakutake was spotted in 1996. It was one of the brightest comets ever seen. It had a long, blue ion tail. Hyakutake Yuji discovered the comet through his binoculars.

A German telescope captured this image of Hyakutake.

Comet Swift-Tuttle

Swift-Tuttle is a large comet. It takes 133 years to orbit the sun. Its dust tail has thousands of meteoroids in it. This is the source of the Perseids meteor shower. It happens when Earth passes through Swift-Tuttle's tail.

The Perseids meteor shower happens each August.

Encke remains fairly close to the sun.

Comet Encke

Encke is a periodic comet. It has the shortest orbit of any known comet. It takes just 3.3 years to orbit the sun. It is 3 miles (4.8 km) across. Encke's tail creates the Taurid meteor shower. This group of meteors appears every fall.

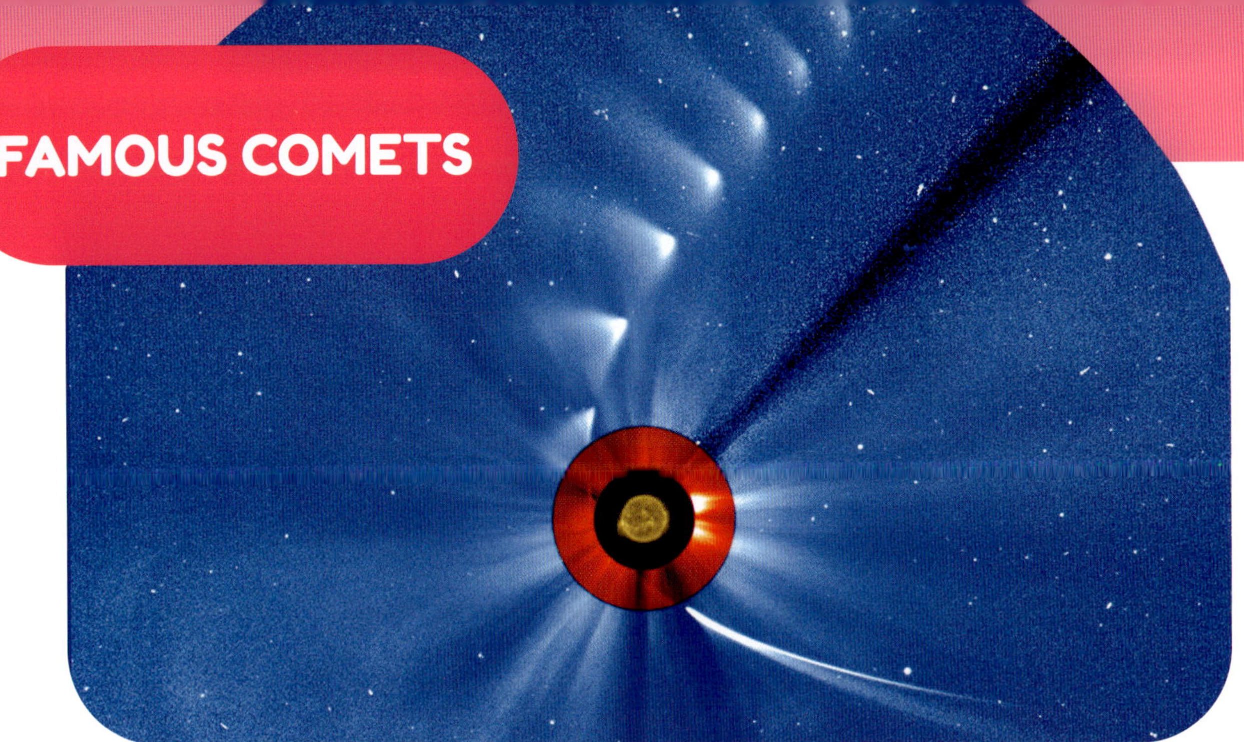

NASA images show ISON coming toward the sun, *bottom right*, and then moving away, *top right*.

Sungrazers

Comets that get very close to the sun are called sungrazers. Some sungrazers fly into the sun. Many others burn up as they get close.

Comet ISON

Comet ISON was seen in 2013. The comet was a sungrazer. It got close to the sun. The comet heated up and tore apart. Scientists across the world worked together to study it. It was the largest organized study of a comet in history.

Comet Bernardinelli-Bernstein

Bernardinelli-Bernstein was discovered in 2021. Scientists think it is the largest comet ever seen. It may be up to 124 miles (200 km) across. This is ten times larger than an average comet.

Bernardinelli-Bernstein was discovered in this telescope image.

Comet Siding Spring

The comet Siding Spring almost hit Mars in 2014. Spacecraft on and near the planet studied it. Scientists believe the comet came from the Oort Cloud. They figured it would not pass by Earth again for another 740,000 years.

NASA changed the orbits of its spacecraft around Mars to protect against dust from Siding Spring.

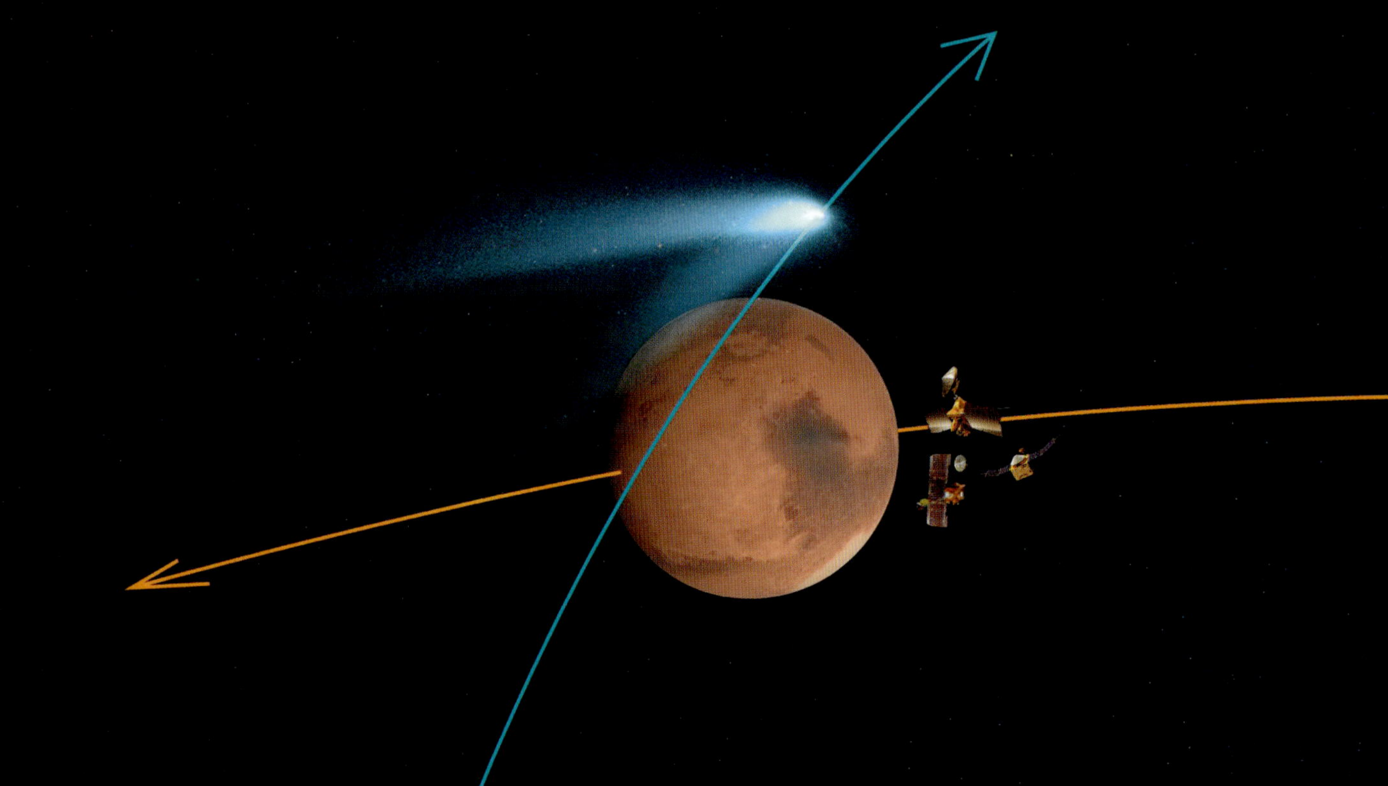

'Oumuamua was spotted as it was leaving the solar system.

FUN FACT!

'Oumuamua means "a messenger from afar arriving first" in Hawaiian.

'Oumuamua

'Oumuamua came from another star system. It was the first known outside object to visit the solar system. It is long and skinny. Objects in the solar system are not shaped this way. Scientists briefly thought it was an asteroid. But further study found it behaved more like a comet.

One Object, Three Names

When a small rock is in space, it is called a meteoroid. When it burns up in Earth's atmosphere, it is a meteor. And when it lands on Earth, it is known as a meteorite.

Meteoroid to Meteorite

Meteors have three names. They change names depending on where they are found.

Meteoroid

Meteor

Meteorite

Meteoroids

Meteoroids are space objects. They can be as little as a grain of dust. They can be as large as a small asteroid. Most meteoroids are pieces of larger objects. Some are pieces of Mars or the moon.

Meteors may travel at more than 25,000 miles per hour (40,200 km/h).

Falling to Earth

Some meteoroids fall into Earth's atmosphere. They are moving very fast. The meteoroids heat up when they run into air. They start to melt.

Shooting Stars

This process heats the air up too. It creates light. The meteor continues to move toward Earth. It leaves a burning trail of light. This is why people call meteors *shooting stars*.

Thousands of meteors shoot across the sky each day.

Meteorite Basics

Small meteors often burn up completely in the atmosphere. There is nothing left of them. But if they are large, they do not totally burn up. Parts fall to the ground. These parts are meteorites.

Searching for meteorites is a hobby for some people.

A meteorite's fall through the atmosphere affects how it looks.

What Do Meteorites Look Like?

Meteorites look like dark rocks. They are burned on the surface. Many look shiny. Some are rough. Others are smooth. Some have a thumbprint-like pattern.

Meteoroid Substances

Many meteoroid substances are similar to asteroid substances. This is because most meteors started as parts of asteroids. They have the same substances as the objects that broke apart.

Stony Meteoroids

Most meteoroids are stony. They are made of silicate rock. Stony meteoroids are lighter than metal ones. They break apart more easily too. Most stony meteoroids contain hardened lava rock. Others do not have lava rock. They come from Mars and the moon. These types of meteoroids are very rare.

Space Weathering

Space objects crash into each other. They create craters. Pieces break off. This type of wear is called space weathering.

This stony meteorite was found in Algeria.

Nickel-Iron Meteoroids

Some meteoroids contain nickel and iron. They are heavy and large. Scientists think nickel-iron meteoroids are pieces of old asteroid cores. About 5 percent of meteorites that reach Earth are nickel-iron. They are heavier than most rocks on Earth.

Nickel-iron meteorites are dark in color.

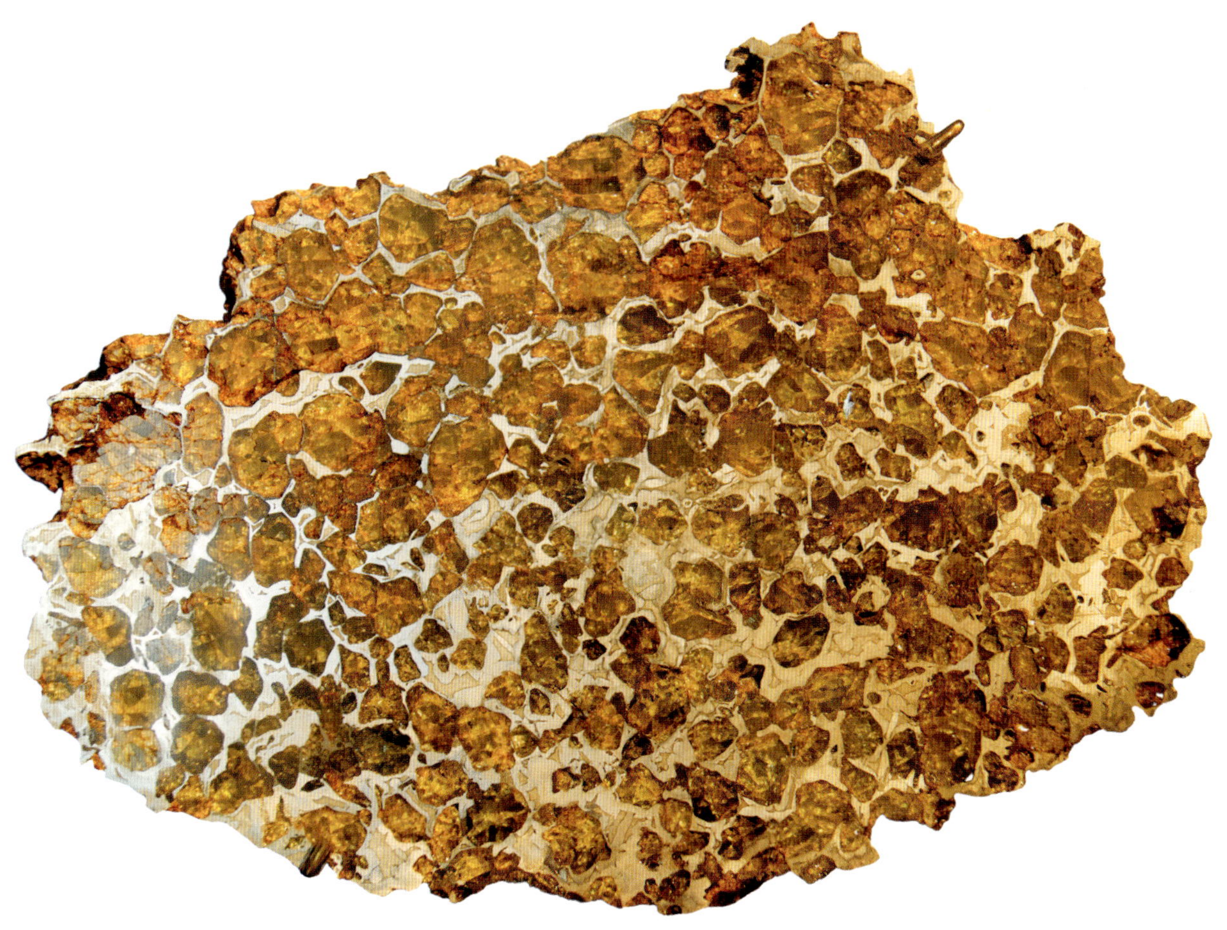

Stony-iron meteorites are popular among collectors.

Stony-Iron Meteoroids

Stony-iron meteoroids have silicate rock. They also have nickel-iron. They have these things in equal parts. Some even contain precious gems and crystals. They are often beautiful.

The Ivuna carbonaceous meteorite fell to Earth in 1938.

Carbonaceous Meteoroids

Carbonaceous meteoroids are very rare. They formed far from the sun. They date back to the start of the solar system. These meteoroids contain carbon and other substances. These substances are the building blocks of life.

Meteoroid Origins

Meteoroids are found throughout the solar system. They orbit the sun. Some are in the inner solar system. Others are near Jupiter, Saturn, and Neptune. They are found in the Kuiper Belt and Oort Cloud too.

Tiny meteoroids are called micrometeoroids.

The solar system is home to countless small meteoroids.

Meteoroids from Comets

Some meteoroids come from comets. Comets have dust tails. These dust tails can contain thousands of meteoroids. They follow the comet through space. They move together. This is called a meteoroid stream.

A comet's dust tail leaves many small pieces behind.

Meteoroids from Asteroids

Asteroids often crash into each other. When they do, pieces fall off. The pieces fly out into the solar system. These pieces are meteoroids. Some meteoroids follow the orbit of their original asteroid. Others get knocked onto a different path. The new path might cross the orbit of a planet.

Scientists closely study meteorites from Mars.

Meteoroids from Mars

Asteroids can crash into Mars. When they do, parts of Mars might get thrown into space. These parts become meteoroids. Scientists can tell when a meteorite is from Mars. Martian meteorites have gases found on Mars.

Meteoroids from the Moon

Asteroids can also crash into the moon. Parts of the moon might get blasted into space. These meteoroids can fall to Earth. Scientists know these meteorites are from the moon. They compare them with rocks that astronauts brought back from the moon.

Private collectors own some meteorites from the moon.

Burning Up

When meteors hit Earth's atmosphere, the air slows them down. This creates lots of heat. The heat causes the meteor to glow. Most meteors burn up in the atmosphere. They do not reach Earth.

Pushing through the atmosphere rapidly slows down a meteor.

Famous Meteor Showers

Several well-known meteor showers occur every year.

Meteor Shower	Time	Meteors per Hour	Parent Comet
Lyrids	April	About 18	Comet C/1861 G1
Eta Aquarids	April–May	About 50	Comet 1P/Halley
Perseids	July–August	About 100	Comet 109P/Swift-Tuttle
Orionids	October–November	About 20	Comet 1P/Halley
Taurids	October–December	About 5	Comet 2P/Encke
Leonids	November–December	About 15	Comet 55P/Tempel-Tuttle

Meteor Showers

Meteors are always falling through the atmosphere. People can observe them each night. When many fall in a short time, it is a meteor shower. Many meteor showers occur at the same time each year. This happens when Earth passes through a comet's meteoroid stream.

A fireball is brighter than the average meteor.

Fireballs

Fireballs are very bright meteors. They appear brighter in the night sky than Venus does. Meteors that cause fireballs are usually large. They can be over 3 feet (1 m) in size.

Too Small to Land

Fireballs are large meteors. But they are not big enough to survive Earth's atmosphere. Fireballs usually break up in the air. Small pieces may reach the ground.

A spacecraft took this image of a fireball from above.

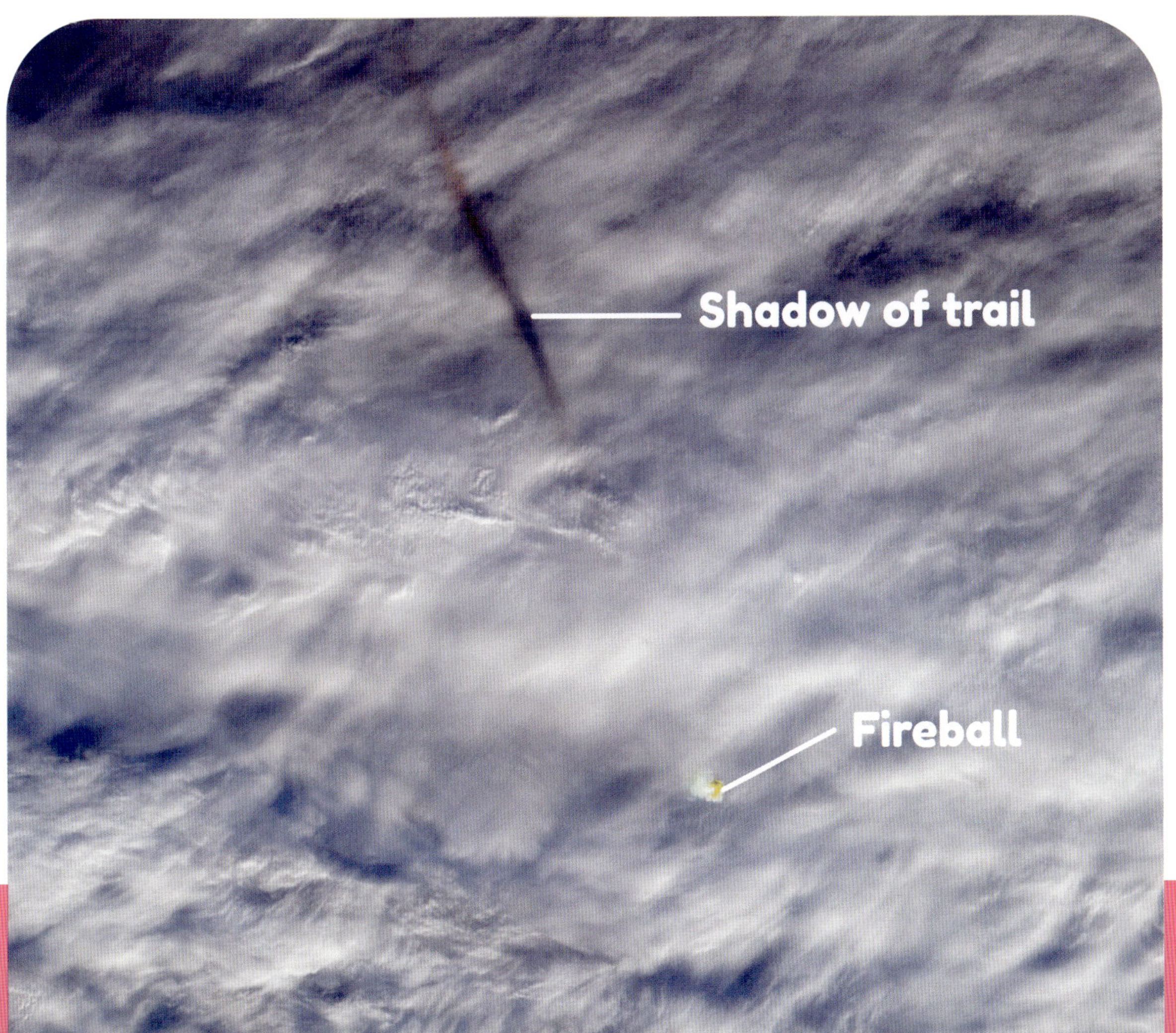

Bolides

Bolides are very large meteors. They explode in the atmosphere before they reach the ground. The explosions are very powerful. They can cause harm on Earth. Animals and people may be injured or killed. Buildings and crops may be destroyed.

Large bolides can cause serious harm. But these strikes are rare.

Nearly Gone

When they reach the surface, most meteorites are small. They are just a tiny part of the original meteor. Most of the meteor is gone. It was burned up. Many meteorites are the size of a pebble. Very few are larger than a fist.

FUN FACT!

Scientists say 48.5 short tons (44 metric tons) of meteors fall on Earth every day.

Many meteorites have been found in Chile's Atacama Desert.

Asteroid Meteorites

More than 50,000 meteorites have been found on Earth. Nearly all of them are from asteroids. Scientists know this because they are made up of the same substances as asteroids.

Lunar and Martian Meteorites

Meteorites from Mars and the moon are much rarer. By April 2025, there were 398 known Martian meteorites. There were 736 known lunar meteorites.

Spotting Meteorites

Meteorites look similar to Earth's rocks. They are easier to see in deserts. Their dark surfaces stand out against the light sand.

A museum in Oman put a Martian meteorite on display.

Sayh al Uhaymir 094
Meteorite from Mars

Meteorites Tell Solar System History

Meteorites help scientists understand the solar system. Many are very old. They provide a window into the early solar system. Scientists can learn how planets formed.

For many years, scientists have studied meteorites with powerful microscopes.

A scientist studies the inner layers of a large meteorite sample.

Meteorites Tell How Earth Formed

Meteorites can also teach scientists about Earth's history. The substances in a meteorite may be similar to those inside Earth. Meteorites help scientists understand Earth's core. Earth likely has a core of nickel-iron. This is the same substance as in nickel-iron meteorites.

Long ago, the powerful gravity of Jupiter and Saturn sent asteroids into the inner solar system.

The Late Heavy Bombardment

Four billion years ago, something changed in the solar system. The orbits of Jupiter, Saturn, Uranus, and Neptune shifted. This moved asteroids out of the asteroid belt. Many asteroids hit Earth. This period lasted up to 200 million years. Scientists call it the Late Heavy Bombardment (LHB).

Meteors and Life

Asteroids and meteorites affected Earth during the LHB. They may have killed off life on the planet. Life may have started again deep in the ocean. This would have protected it from meteorite crashes.

The LHB affected both Earth and the moon.

Chelyabinsk Meteor

In 2013, a fireball streaked across the sky. It happened over Chelyabinsk, Russia. The fireball was the size of a house. It exploded 14 miles (23 km) above the ground. The explosion gave off a lot of energy. The blast blew out windows across a wide area. More than 1,600 people were injured.

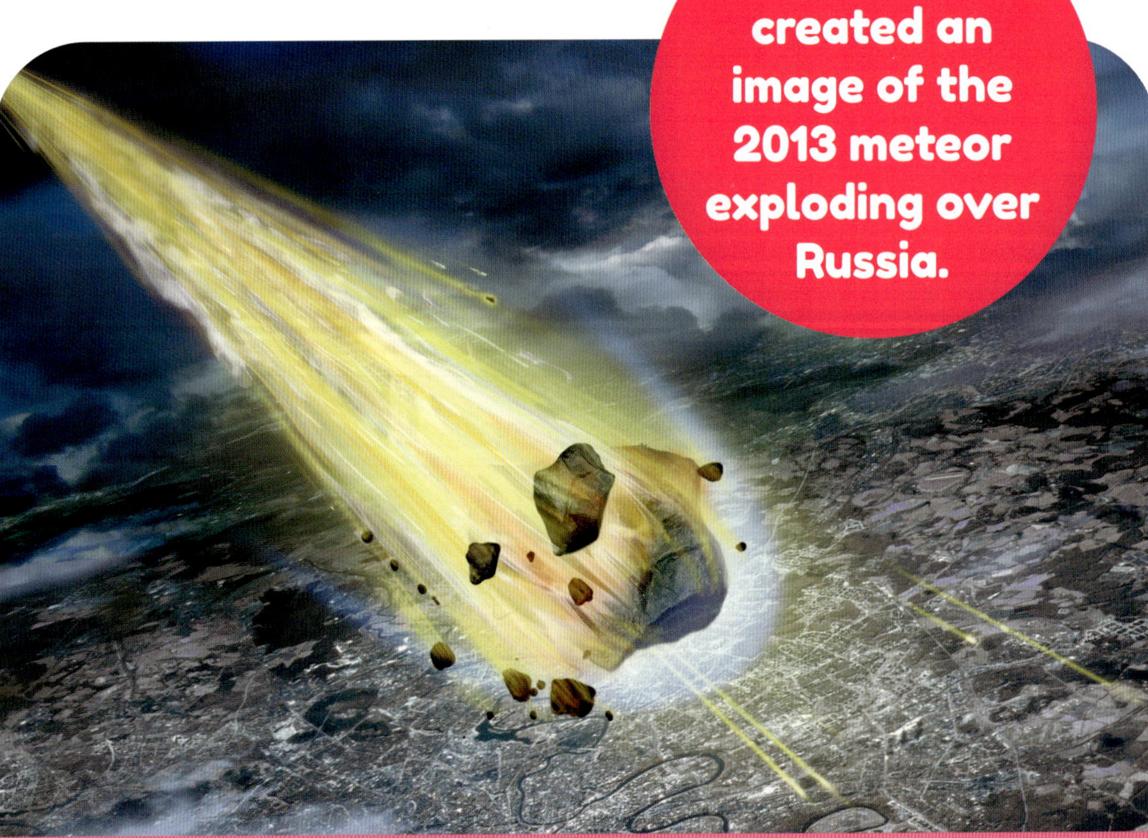

An artist created an image of the 2013 meteor exploding over Russia.

The Tunguska Event

In 1908, a meteor fell over Siberia in Russia. Scientists think it was 120 feet (37 m) across. It was the largest meteor in modern history. It exploded in the air miles above the ground. The explosion was very powerful. It knocked over trees across hundreds of miles.

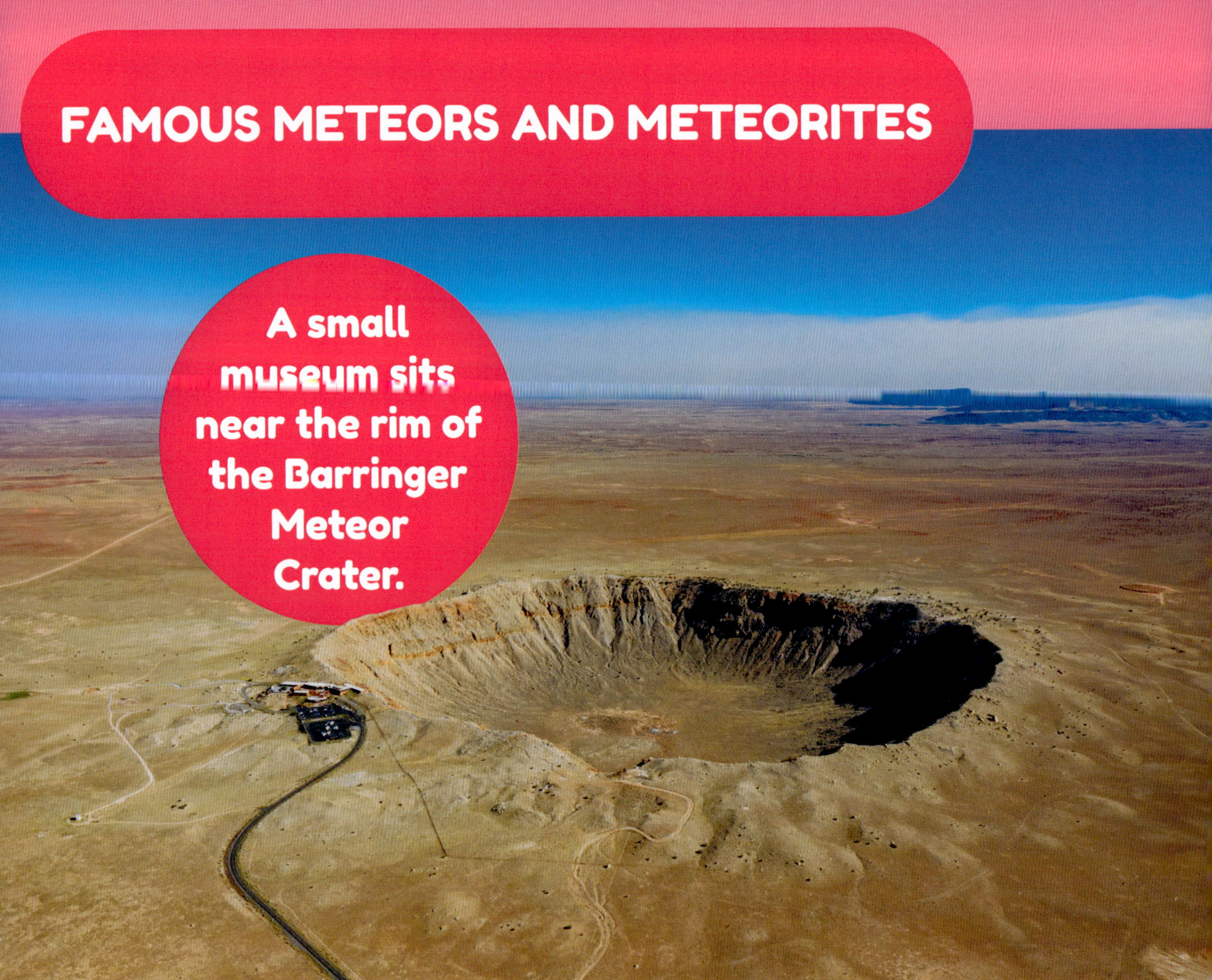

A small museum sits near the rim of the Barringer Meteor Crater.

Barringer Meteor Crater

The Barringer Meteor Crater is in Arizona. It is 0.6 miles (1 km) across. It formed when a meteorite hit Earth. This happened 50,000 years ago. The meteorite was made of nickel-iron. It was 164 feet (50 m) across.

Chicxulub Crater

The Chicxulub meteorite fell to Earth 65 million years ago. It left a huge crater on the Yucatán Peninsula in Mexico. The crater is 180 miles (290 km) wide. The crash killed off most animals on Earth. This included the dinosaurs.

Scientists think the Chicxulub meteorite was about 6 miles (9.7 km) wide.

Manicouagan Crater

The Manicouagan Crater is in Quebec, Canada. Scientists think a meteorite 3 miles (4.8 km) in diameter created the crater. It crashed into Earth 215.5 million years ago. This was during the Triassic Period. The first dinosaurs appeared around this time.

Images from space show the huge Manicouagan Crater.

Multiple Rings

The Manicouagan Crater has multiple rings. The rings span 60 miles (97 km) across. There is a lake in the middle. The lake is 40 miles (64 km) across. In the middle of the lake is a large island.

Visitors can touch the Hoba meteorite.

Hoba Meteorite

The Hoba meteorite is the largest ever found on Earth. It is in Namibia. Scientists first described it in 1920. The Hoba meteorite weighs about 119,000 pounds (54,000 kg). It is still in the place where it landed on Earth 80,000 years ago.

Peekskill Meteorite

The Peekskill meteorite crashed down to Earth in October 1992. It was the size of a bowling ball. It crashed into the trunk of a parked car in New York State. It went through the trunk and dented the driveway. People who saw it said the meteorite smelled of sulfur.

The car hit by the Peekskill meteorite was later shown in museums.

Allende Meteorite

The Allende meteorite fell over Pueblito de Allende, Mexico, in 1969. It exploded into pieces. The pieces fell to Earth over more than 116 square miles (300 sq km). This is one of the largest meteorite trails ever recorded.

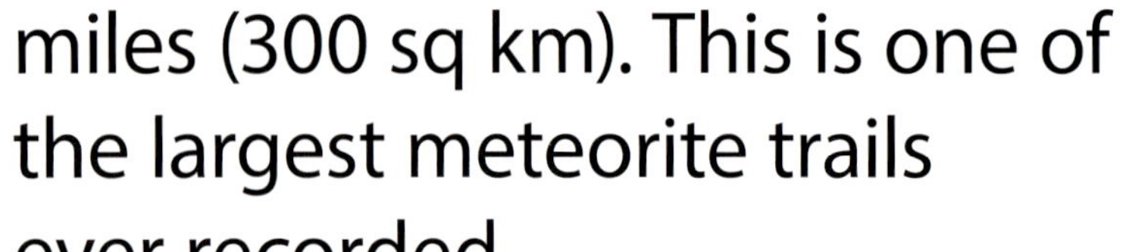

A slice of the Allende meteorite was displayed at Arizona State University.

A NASA scientist experiments with a piece of dust from the Allende meteorite.

Collecting Meteorites

Scientists and local schoolchildren visited the Allende meteorite site. They carefully walked across the land. They collected pieces of meteorite. The smallest piece weighed 0.04 ounces (1 g). The largest weighed 242 pounds (110 kg).

An old illustration shows where the Ensisheim meteorite fell to Earth.

Ensisheim Meteorite

One of the earliest recorded meteorite falls happened in 1492. A 280-pound (127 kg) meteorite fell in a field in Ensisheim, France. Maximilian I was the Holy Roman Emperor. He had the meteorite placed in a church.

Willamette Meteorite/ Tomanowos

The Willamette meteorite is the largest ever found in the United States. It weighs 15.5 short tons (14 metric tons). It is made of iron. The American Indian Clackamas people have known about the meteorite for centuries. They call it Tomanowos.

Healing Meteorite

Rain collects in the dents on Tomanowos's surface. The Clackamas people believe this rainwater has healing powers.

Children play on the Willamette meteorite in the 1930s.

GLOSSARY

atmosphere
The gases that surround an object in space.

basaltic
Relating to rock formed by magma.

contain
To hold or have within.

dwarf planet
An object that orbits the sun and is ball-shaped but is not big enough to change the orbits of other objects.

gravity
A force that objects have that pulls at other objects.

hydrocarbon
A substance made of just carbon and hydrogen.

injured
Hurt.

lunar
Related to the moon.

Martian
Related to the planet Mars.

mission
A task or job.

orbit
To follow a curved path around another object.

particle
A tiny piece of something.

silicate
A substance made of metal, silicon, and oxygen.

solar system
The sun along with all the planets, moons, and other bodies that orbit it.

substance
What something is made of.

volcanic
Relating to a vent in the crust of a planet where hot rock leaks out.

TO LEARN MORE

More Books to Read

Bullard, Lisa. *The Planets*. Abdo, 2026.

LaPierre, Yvette. *The Asteroid Belt*. ReferencePoint, 2023.

Strother, Ruth. *Outer Space*. Silver Dolphin, 2021.

Online Resources

To learn more about asteroids, comets, and meteors, please visit **abdobooklinks.com** or scan this QR code. These links are routinely monitored and updated to provide the most current information available.

INDEX

PHOTO CREDITS

Cover Photos: Marko Aliaksandr/Shutterstock Images, front; Adobe Stock, back

Interior Photos: Dotted Yeti/Shutterstock Images, 1, 8, 86 (meteoroid); Akito Studio/Shutterstock Images, 3; NASA, 4, 10, 11, 15, 18 (bottom), 22, 23, 29, 34–35, 36, 40, 41 (bottom), 42, 45 (bottom), 48, 49, 50, 53, 59, 60 (top), 61, 66, 73, 78, 80, 82 (top), 84, 100, 105, 111, 123; Shutterstock Images, 5, 13, 18 (top), 20, 25, 26, 27 (top), 28, 30, 33 (bottom), 37, 38, 39 (bottom), 41 (top), 45 (top), 52, 54, 55, 56, 57, 60 (bottom), 62, 71, 72, 81, 82 (bottom), 87, 88, 89, 91, 92, 93 (top), 97, 98, 102, 104, 107, 108, 109 (top), 112, 118, 125 (top); AstroStar/Shutterstock Images, 6; NorthSky Films/Shutterstock Images, 7; Pavel Chagochkin/Shutterstock Images, 9; ESO, 12, 44, 85; NASA/Newsmakers/Getty Images, 14; ESA, 16, 58; Henning Dalhoff/Bonnier Publications/Science Source, 17; Ian Cuming/Science Source, 19; Vicor Habbick Visions/Science Photo Library/Alamy, 21; Mark Garlick/Science Source, 24, 33 (top), 39 (top); Red Line Editorial, 27 (bottom), 43, 103; Guido Vermeulen-Perdaen/Shutterstock Images, 31; Elias H. Debbas II/Shutterstock Images, 32; L. Calçada/M. Kornmesser/Nick Risinger/JAXA/ESO, 46; DLR German Aerospace Center, 47; Chris Butler/Science Source, 51; Diego Rebello/Shutterstock Images, 63; Detlev van Ravenswaay/Science Source, 64, 106, 115, 124; Nicole R. Fuller/Science Source, 65; John R. Foster/Science Source, 67, 77; Tim Brown/Science Source, 68; Ron Miller/Science Source, 69, 113, 114; Johan Swanepoel/Shutterstock Images, 70; Dr. H. S. Banton/Science Source, 74; Marcel Clemens/Shutterstock Images, 75; Julian Baum/Science Source, 76; Landessternwarte Heidelberg-Königstuhl, 79; National Optical-Infrared Astronomy Research Laboratory, 83; Vadim Sadovski/Shutterstock Images, 86 (meteor); Marina Kryuchina/Shutterstock Images, 86 (meteorite), 90; Susan E. Degginger/Science Source, 93 (bottom); Joyce Photographics/Science Source, 94; Mark Williamson/Science Source, 95; The Natural History Museum, London/Science Source, 96; Photon Illustration/Stocktrek Images/Science Source, 99; Steve Jurvetson/Wikimedia, 101; Mohammed Mahjoub/AFP/Getty Images, 109 (bottom); Lucinda Douglas-Menzies/Science Source, 110; Kit Leong/Shutterstock Images, 116; Jurik Peter/Shutterstock Images, 117; Ovidiu Minoiu/Shutterstock Images, 119; Jiri Balek/Shutterstock Images, 120; Ingo Wagner dpa/Picture Alliance/Getty Images, 121; Wikimedia Commons, 122; Bettmann/Getty Images, 125 (bottom)